SOCIAL CHANGE IN WESTERN EUROPE

SMALL AND MEDIUM-SIZE ENTERPRISES

edited by
ARNALDO BAGNASCO
and
CHARLES F. SABEL

PINTER

PINTER
A Cassell Imprint
Wellington House, 125 Strand, London WC2R 0BB, England

First published in Great Britain in 1995

British Library Cataloguing in Publication Data

A CIP catalogue record for this book is available from the British Library

ISBN 1 85567 305 3 (hb)
    1 85567 306 1 (pb)

Typeset by Saxon Graphics Ltd, Derby
Printed and bound in Great Britain

SOCIAL CHANGE IN WESTERN EUROPE

SMALL AND MEDIUM-SIZE ENTERPRISES

The *Social Change in Western Europe* series developed from the need to provide a summary of current thinking from leading academic thinkers on major social and economic issues concerning the evolving policies of Western Europe in the post-Maastricht era. To create an effective European Union governments and politicians throughout the region must work to provide satisfactory social, economic and political conditions for the populations of Europe, and each volume affords an opportunity to look at specific issues and their impact on individual countries.

The series is directed by an academic committee composed of Arnaldo Bagnasco (Turin University), Henri Mendras (CNRS, Paris) and Vincent Wright (Nuffield, Oxford), assisted by Patrick Le Galès (CNRS, Rennes), Anand Menon (University of Oxford) with the support of Michel Roger and Olivier Cazenave (Futuroscope in Poitiers). This group forms the *Observatoire du Changement en Europe Occidentale* which was launched in Poitiers (France) in 1990 with the generous funding of the Fondation de Poitiers headed by René Monory.

SOCIAL CHANGE IN WESTERN EUROPE

IN THE SAME SERIES

CONTENTS

LIST OF CONTRIBUTORS

Arnaldo Bagnasco is a sociologist and Professor at the University of Turin, with a special interest in the regionalisation of social structures and smaller enterprises as well as in urban sociology. Among other studies he has published *Tre Italie: la problematica territoriale dello sviluppo italiano* (1977), Bologna, Il Mulino; (with C. Trigilia) *La construction sociale du marché: le défi de la troisième Italie* (1993), Cachan; (with N. Negri) *Classi, Leti, Personne: esercizi d'analisi sociale localizzata* (1994), Naples, Liguori. He is co-editor of the review *Stato e Mercato*.

Sebastiano Brusco is Professor of Industrial Economy at the University of Modena. Among his publications are: *Agricoltora ricca e classi sociali* (1979), Milan, Feltrinelli; *Piccole imprese e distretti industriali* (1989), Turin, Rosenberg & Sellier.

Juan José Castillo is Professor of Sociology at the Complutense University of Madrid, and editor of the review *Sociologia del trabajo*. He has conducted a number of surveys on Spanish firms and has published *Informatizacion, trabajo y empleo en las pequenas empresas espanolas* (1991); *La division del trabajo entre empresas* (1989); and (ed.) *Las nuevas formes de organizacion del trabajo* (1987).

Bernard Ganne is a sociologist and Director of Research at CNRS (*Glysi: Groupe lyonnais de sociologie industrielle*) studying urban development and industrial activity. He has published *Gens de cuir, gens de papier* (1983), CNRS; 'Place et évolution des systèmes industriels locaux en France' (1992), in G. Benko and A. Lipietz *Des Régions qui gagnent*, Paris, PUF; *Industrialisation diffuse et systèmes industriels localisés: essai de bibliographie critique du cas français* (1990), ILO, Geneva.

He is extending the field of his research to include Italy, the UK and African countries.

Peer Hull Kristensen is Associate Professor at the Institute of Organisation and Industrial Sociology at the Copenhagen Business School. He has recently published several articles dealing with industrial transformation and reorganisation in Denmark.

Charles F. Sabel is Professor of Social Sciences at the Massachusetts Institute of Technology. In addition to numerous articles, he has published *Work and Politics* (1982); and (with Michael Piore) *The Second Industrial Divide* (1985), New York, Basic Books.

Klaus Semlinger is Professor of the Sociology of Labour at the Fachhochschule für Technik und Wirstschaft in Berlin, after previously working at the Institute of Social Sciences in Münich. He is the author of several studies and articles including (with G. Schmid) *Arbeitsmarktpolitik fur Behinderte* (1985), Bale, Boston, Stuttgart, Birkhaüser; (ed.) *Staatliche Intervention durch Dienstleistungen – Funktionsweise und Steurrungspotential* (1988), Berlin, Sigma; and *Flexibilisierung des Arbeitsmarktes – Interessen, Wirkungen, Perspektiven* (1991), Frankfurt, New York, Campus.

Carlo Trigilia is Professor of Economic Sociology at the University of Florence and co-editor of the review *Stato e Mercato*. His studies concern economic development. His publications include *Grandi partiti e piccolo imprese* (1986), Bologna, Il Mulino; *Sviluppo senza autonomia. Effeti perversi delle politiche nel Mezzogiorno* (1992), Bologna, Il Mulino; and (with A. Bagnasco) *La construction sociale du marché: le défi de la troisième Italie* (1993), Cachan.

Jonathan Zeitlin is Associate Professor of Industrial Relations at Madison College, University of Wisconsin, following a period in London and Cambridge. He is the author of (with Steven Tolliday) *The Power to Manage? Employers and Industrial Relations in Comparative Historical Perspective* (1991), London and New York, Routledge; (with Paul Hirst) *Reversing Industrial Decline? Industrial Structure and Policy in Britain and her Competitors* (1989), Oxford, Berg, New York, St Martins; and (with Steven Tolliday) *Between Fordism and Flexibility: The Automobile Industry and its Workers* (1992) (2nd ed.), Oxford, Berg, and New York, St Martins.

INTRODUCTION: AN UNEXPECTED AND CONTROVERSIAL RETURN

ARNALDO BAGNASCO*

The start of the story

Perhaps it is not such a bad idea that the first person to commence this book is an Italian. For Italy is one of the first European countries in which a process, that was later to become generalised, was present and relatively consolidated by the late 1960s. The process to which I refer is the major new contribution made by small and medium-sized firms to the contemporary economy. The author of this introduction has worked in one of the places in which the story we shall be telling, whose significance we shall be discussing and the follow-up to which we shall try to imagine, actually started. Like anyone else who has worked in one of these places, he has had the advantage of observing the phenomena which interest us here right from the outset. On the other hand, however much he has surveyed the scene around him and sought to reason in general terms, he also suffers the disadvantage of being influenced by a specific viewpoint over the entire question. This is an important fact to bear in mind.

Every country – that is every national economy – has its own start to the story. In the UK it came with the oft-neglected work of the Boltom Commission, set up to investigate the small-firm sector. Little was known about the latter at that point in time, save for the fact that it was in evident difficulty. The Commission presented its findings in 1971 and published them the following year. They

* The author would like to express his appreciation to John Irving who translated this text from the original Italian.

showed that the UK had the lowest number of small firms of any industrialised nation. Using the conventional classificatory ceiling of 200 employees, the number of the people employed in firms of this size accounted for 22 per cent of the total of employees in industry. At the opposite end of the scale came Italy with 66 per cent. All the other countries were somewhere in between.

It is of no interest to us here to recall the other findings of the survey, less still how they were interpreted or the recommendations which accompanied them. Today we tend to be somewhat critical of them, although we are prepared to acknowledge that they heralded renewed political and scientific attention to the phenomenon in question. What does interest us though is the idea that the UK and Italy can be imagined at opposite ends of a scale.

The percentages cited hide a miscellany of situations: from small traditional craftsmen struggling to survive in the face of mass production to high-quality craftsmen with secure markets, from small firms working at dirt-cheap prices as subsuppliers to small firms with excellent technology and rich insterstitial markets. In part, Italy's 66 per cent already comprised the vanguard movement of the small firms' return to the economic scene. During those years researchers were beginning to note the phenomenon – and to be surprised by its force.

The two points at either end of the scale may thus be expressed in the following terms. In the UK the Boltom Report begged the question: 'How can we avoid losing small firms and what can we do to increase their number?' In Italy, however the question asked was: 'How can we explain the development of whole regions, now rising to the apex of national wealth, based exclusively on small firms?'

The two questions were prompted by reality. Initially, at least, they presupposed the existence of different problems and attention to different institutional questions. The British question made immediate reference to politics and its capacity to support growth. The Italian question had to do with the spontaneity of the process, drawing attention to the social and cultural features which made growth possible in some regions and not in others, without it being planned by regional policy or even forecast at all. Of course, lurking behind both questions was the more directly economic issue of the scope granted to small firms in the contemporary economy.

One of the criticisms that was subsequently directed at the Boltom Commission was that in its recommendations it neglected the influence of initial social and cultural conditions and their capacity to support or block any development process based on small firms. On the other hand, as we shall see, politics eventually also assumed an increasingly important role in the Italian case. With the benefit of hindsight, it is possible to argue that anyone observing the two countries together would have caught sight of the different institutional factors at play. From case to case, they combined in different ways with varying degrees of success, sometimes even changing combination in the course of time.

This is the path I intend to follow here: it is the one we have followed over years of research. It even helps us to frame the various national starting-points. It is possible, for example, to say that the French case is similar to the British one, perhaps slightly nearer to the centre of the scale. The recent Spanish case is, instead, close to the Italian one, albeit materialising years later. Is it fair to add that the case of Baden-Württemberg, with its bottom-up momentum and its wealth of public and private back-up organisations, belongs halfway along the scale?

The exercise could be continued with other examples, although, of course, metaphors are valid only up to a point. They let us see some things and they hide others. In our case, the quantitative scale metaphor tends to hide qualitative differences. Directly connected to this question is another – that of the strong, albeit generic expectation of policies 'for the small firm'. At this stage it is a good idea to clear up a few preliminary points.

Today no one is prepared any longer to question the capacity of minor firms to create wealth and employment even in the modern economy – which is precisely why students of the phenomenon and public authorities are expected to come up with easy recipes to support them and, more important, to make them appear where they are still non-existent by imitating processes which have taken place elsewhere.

Researchers must be on their guard against over-simplistic ideas in this respect. On the one hand, they have worked towards a general theory of forms of development based on small firms which can undoubtedly offer suggestions on how to act. On the other, however, they have also observed the highly varied manifestations of the phenomena. Thus, it may be possible to plot a straight line to give an idea of general trends, but there is great dispersion of dots around it. This is why it is impossible to come up with easy solutions. Nonetheless, comparison of a certain situation with others is one way – probably the only reasonable way – of imagining which resources may be mobilised in other cases and which obstacles must be overcome to achieve results. The point is that obstacles and resources generally appear in different forms in different cases.

Second, and starting to go into greater detail, it is by no means clear whether those who converse about small and medium-sized firms are addressing the same problem, simply because the small firm is not a subject for analysis but, as they say, a residual category. Insofar as it is inherently small – which is how economists have seen it – it is merely the opposite of large.

What many researchers have in common is the idea that over recent years there have been cases of local and regional development according to patterns not envisaged by traditional economic theory, which has focused its attention on industrial concentration processes and increasingly rootless industry. Nevertheless, the difficulties of such theories, and, above all, the difficulties experienced by large industrial firms in the not too distant past are no guarantee that there has been only one response in terms of small and medium-sized firms. In a certain sense, we return here to the previous point, but with a proviso: it is necessary to clarify which types of small firms and which forms of inter-firm relations are to be included and which are to be excluded or treated separately as belonging to different economic logics. Returning to the statistical analogy made above, not only are the dots representing the different cases of small firms widely dispersed: there may also be more than one straight line around which they tend to align.

There is a third point worth stressing, and perhaps a decisive one in terms of the choice of path to take. In the best studies the question of small firms has never been distinguished from that of large ones. The traditional approach was to study the systematic relationships between large industrial firms and their subsuppliers. The new development has been the return of production systems based exclusively on small and medium-sized firms. To what extent could they be regarded as autonomous? Were they to be considered very old or very new? Were they going to last? Was the conflict between dispersed production and centralised production – fought out during the beginnings of modern capitalism and won by large-scale production – breaking out once more? Dispersed production was gaining new leeway; how much, exactly, it was hard to say.

Leaving aside for the moment relations between large-scale industrial firms and small subsuppliers, which were also develop-

ing into new forms of collaboration with varying degrees of subor-
dination, the most interesting new development was, nonetheless,
the growth of local systems of industrial production based on small
and medium-sized firms. This has been the subject of much of the
research carried out on small firms, influenced no doubt by the
particularity of the Italian case. Widening the perspective in the
opposite direction – although by doing so perhaps one risks
sounding somewhat vague – it is possible at best to suggest the
following formulation: what are the economic and social, exoge-
nous and endogenous, conditions which explain the birth and
transformation of local economies in which small firms count a lot,
are relatively independent and, as a whole, are to a certain extent
capable of strategy?

Basically, this is the theme of my introduction, which will be
divided into two parts. In the first part we shall consider history
and theory. In the second, we shall examine some national cases to
try to understand the different positions occupied by small and
medium-sized firms, especially in those regions where they count a
great deal in the sense indicated above; each country is capable
through its peculiarities of throwing light on a particular aspect of
the general problem. In this way, we shall return once more to
theory. We may even be able to attempt some well-founded forecast. It should be noted that our approach is that of a seminar in
the true sense of the word insofar as it presents and discusses
different cases and positions against a theoretical horizon which
does not presuppose one single – or not necessarily one single –
predetermined conclusion.

The social construction of the market: industrial districts

Therefore to Italy let us return – to Italy as it was fifteen or twenty
years ago, during the golden age of the industrial districts of small
firms in the central and north-eastern regions of the country. Now,
years on, analytical tools have been greatly refined and the particularities of the case are becoming increasingly clear, although some
of the conclusions made at the time allowed interpretative
elements of a more general order to emerge. Some of them I have
anticipated: now it is necessary to elaborate them.

First, it was evident from the outset that in order to understand
the growth of certain villages, towns and regions, it was necessary
to view them both from within and without. Large-scale industry

was clearly in difficulty, whereas small industry was beginning to enjoy a period of great economic buoyancy. This is not an obvious fact in itself; it begs questions as to the relations, direct or indirect, between large and small industry.

The phenomenon could be explained through large industry's decentralisation of production in pursuit of more favourable cost and labour management conditions. This, in turn, is not obvious since – as was noted at the time – it presupposes that technological conditions and organisational solutions existed which made decentralisation competitive with respect to concentration, in terms of product and process quality and reliability. Thus, it was necessary to cease thinking of small firms as a historical surplus. Attention was soon to shift, therefore, from simple 'decentralisation of production' to a new specialised interfirm division of labour and to the complex interplay of components markets in which different motivations were at work.

However, apart from that a conspicuous and notable fact was that new small firms often belonged to sectors in which large firms had not previously been present. The small Italian firms did not manufacture production cars or chemicals but produced non-standardised consumer goods, ancillary machine tools and investment goods. Therefore, the question that had to be asked was a general one: what are the conditions which create space for non-standardised small-scale production in the contemporary economy? A growing fragmented demand on international markets, better communications networks, new flexible production technologies suitable for small plants – these are general conditions favourable to non-standardised, small-scale production. But this suggests a second question: 'Why in some cities and not others; why in certain regions and not in others?'

If the attention of economists was attracted by industrial districts – that is by the numerous specialised areas of small-scale manufacturers, in which conditions still to be studied made the horizontal as opposed to vertical integration of production advantageous, that of sociologists was drawn to local societies. Industrial districts were activated by societies that were distinguished by characteristic traits. It soon became clear that in order to understand their success it was necessary to study particular forms of integration of the economy in society. It was no coincidence that Karl Polanyi became a reference point for sociologists of small firms, just as Alfred Marshall had for economists.

In these districts the economy seemed to be substantially regulated by the free market. It also seemed possible to speak in terms of a labour market in which staff were recruited and dismissed with ease, and in which there was space for free interpersonal bargaining. Lurking behind bargaining, however, it was possible to glimpse a complicated social construction of the market. Primary cultural and social characteristics permitted diffuse activisation, support and compensation for economic risk, ensuring wide sharing of the advantages and acceptance of the model. The historical legacy of the Italy of the Renaissance city states with their countryside of sharecroppers and peasants, devoid of dispersed mass industrialisation, proved to be precious in activating a new form of diffuse development when circumstances became favourable.

A close-knit fabric of larger and smaller cities well connected one with another had distributed urban functions – banks, schools, industrial estates, services – throughout the territory. In some places craft traditions were strong and dealers often already had a consolidated network of acquaintances and relations abroad. Previous experience of industry and vocational training schools had made basic industrial socialisation available in some places. In the countryside, extended families of independent workers provided support for relatives wishing to offer their services in an initially unstable, low-wage industrial labour market. They did so with unitary strategies which sometimes allowed the individual to set up business on his own. From the organisational, social and cultural point of view, this was a society ready and prepared for the new adventure. The resources available were not exceptionally rich but were well spread out among the population. In town and cities the conditions existed for numerous small accumulations of capital which might reasonably be risked in working shoulder to shoulder with people known for years and with whom there was good understanding.

This is not the place to delve into the knowledge we have accumulated of these processes, not least because these are the most specific aspects of the question. Nonetheless, this need to consider the specific forms of the integration of the economy in society is still the most general approach to the problem. As we shall see, by devoting attention to this problem and not simply to the 'economy' it is possible to understand transformational trends.

One point must be stressed. In Italian districts as well, abstract resemblances cannot hide important differences in the economy and in the societies it corresponds to. An engineering-based district is different from a textile-based one, while a district based on both engineering and textiles is different again. A textile sector in the Veneto is backed by a local society which is, in part, different from Tuscan society. Even if the sectors are the same, the method of function is somewhat different. In the case of clothing, the strategic social actors are dealers and in this sector work is down-graded and paid less. In the furniture sector, the leading role is played by craftsmen, with their skill and interminable working days. Mechanical engineering is often comprised of workers who have set up in business on their own and workers who work a normal timetable and who sometimes have a secondary occupa-tion. In some cases, we enter the world of high technology; in others we find a world of traditional firms in which wages continue to be low. Certain districts are made up of very similar companies: they are born as a result of a processs of imitation and produce the same goods in competition with one another. In other sectors there is a sophisticated inter-firm division of labour. In some cases the internal integration of districts is high; in others numerous firms are part of external production cycles. In some districts the quality of urban life is high; in others less so. In some cases it is distinctly poor. Generally speaking, however, these are the Italian regions in which the services to the population are best developed. It is useful to insist upon differences as well as resemblances since subsequent comparison on an international scale further amplified the framework of possibilities. However, the need to make distinc-tions continued, even when treating a single country.

Thus originally it was possible to see a variety of local societies seeking to adapt to the external environment with their own resources. Some were successful, others less so. Their common matrix was their diffuse capacity to find adaptations of the econ-omy to society 'that worked'. It should be noted that over the years growth was not in general extensive, with a growing number of people involved in a traditional mode of production, but intensive through investment in technology and increased productivity. This was accompanied for a long period by higher wages and the capac-ity to limit the dualistic employment tendencies typical of the small firm economy. All this cannot be explained without knowledge of the particular forms of integration of the economy in society. Is it not a surprise, for example – and also a particularity with respect to other known cases – that it is precisely in these regions that the highest national levels of trade union membership have been recorded?

These last remarks suggest that profound dynamics of transformation have always been at work and that small firm systems have often been capable of strategies in difficult external contexts. This does not preclude the fact that the borderlines between large and small may be mobile; and that the fact is particularly visible in types of production that have never been clear-cut. This too is a generalisable statement.

In the next section we shall seek to establish the modifications to forms of integration of the economy in society which have permitted adaptation to changed conditions. New conditions, of course, regard both the internal context of local societies and the world economic context as a whole. As far as local societies are concerned, a general idea to consider is that while primary social differences are becoming less valid, important new differences have been increasingly established by subsequent adaptations. From this point of view it is necessary to evaluate the durability and vulnerability of the different districts. It is not a good idea to make generalisations on the basis of limited observation. With reference to context, the new development of the 1980s was the renewed strength of large-scale industrial firms. To use a colloquial expression: 'Large-scale industrial firms have come out of their corner'; or, more idiomatically and aggressively, 'oligopolies are doing fine, thank you very much!'

Small firms: the plot thickens

In the preceding section my reasoning was of the 'bottom-up' type. Here I shall start to view things in 'top-bottom' terms and move away from the Italian case to a discussion on a more hypothetical level.

The observations I have made on the new differences that have emerged suggest that today it may be possible to study the phenomena – at least in the developed economies – with the help of more unified conceptual frameworks. The latter enable us to pinpoint processes with which we are still relatively unacquainted. There is no lack of typologies for local production systems, and these are a first step towards possible theoretical interpretations. Here I shall be touching upon only a few aspects of the general framework.

Before looking at large industry, let us return for a moment to primary differences. Starting conditions such as those in the Italian case are really most extraordinary. The more general implications that we have dealt with are somewhat abstract, and it is necessary to beware of falling into traps. Let us demonstrate the point with an example.

A trap we have learnt to avoid regards the development of the generalisable principle whereby to understand the economy it is necessary to understand the forms of its integration in society. Moving one step forward, it has been found that the primary form was the integration of the free market and specific cultural and social traditions capable of activating and compensating for it. Taking another step forward, it might be possible further to specify the analysis by drawing attention to the fundamental point of the reciprocal 'trust' between actors, which is a *conditio sine qua non* for entry into a cooperative market game. As we know, trust is a precious and scarce resource without which market development cannot take root. To a certain extent, the question of trust may appear to be the core of the interpretation.

At this point in the argument, however, the Italian case risks being misleading insofar as it bears out the idea of a sort of great cultural 'reservoir' of trust available and continually supplied throughout traditional society. A corollary of this position might be that, without this reservoir, diffuse economic development is impossible. Both assertions are, however, false because in other cases small firm development has been observed in areas devoid of important cultural reservoirs. Theoretical attention has thus, rightly, shifted to processes which may generate extended fabrics of trust, unavailable in traditional culture, in some cases through market interaction. Hirshmann's warning that the market may either integrate or consume social relations according to circumstances continues to be valid. We are forced to conclude, therefore, that the social construction of the market contemplates a number of structurally diverse solutions.

But let us return to large-scale industrial firms – the oligopolies. They have once more reinforced their position on the scene. They do not enjoy good health everywhere – in Italy, for example. In general, however, they are back in the limelight. There are many reasons for this. What interests us here is the organisational aspect. Internally, rigid old structures have become more flexible, regaining what had once been the advantage of small firms. What is more, new forms of organisation have also entailed transformations in the fabric of small and large-scale firms. One way of addressing the problem is to observe that these changes have been fostered by microelectronic and telematic technologies. The more the latter are disseminated, the more changes we can expect to see. We thus venture on to relatively unexplored ground in which phenomena are in the course of evolving.

The effects of the dissemination of microelectronics in production processes – most typically through the introduction of numeric-control machinery – have been centrifugal; the scope for technical economies of scale has decreased. The introduction of telematics, on the contrary, has had centripetal effects since it facilitates the management of economies of scope with regard to types of product which are technically different but connected from the commercial point of view, and also requires the concentration of governance functions to be viably applicable. The interplay between the two tendencies has heralded the appearance of a new type of organisation: the network-firm characterised by a high concentraton of governance functions (production management, marketing, control) and the dispersion of production functions into hierarchically connected or independent units. The latter, in turn, are linked to the principal firm by more or less stable relations, with different forms of possible organisational integration: long-term agreements, financial holdings, joint ventures, franchising.

The network-firm has both the interest and capacity to invade industrial districts of small manufacturing firms in search of partners. It appears to be doing so in a number of cases. From the point of view of single firms, this may lead to advantages in some cases and losses of margins of autonomy in others. Some small firms may find it hard to bear the economic conditions of participation, with dire repercussions for their cost structures, for example, their capacity to pay wages. Furthermore, it is expensive to leave the network once you are a part of it. From the district's point of view the long-term risk will be one of possible disarticulation.

It is unclear what may happen sector by sector, district by district, and according to the the type of interfirm relations existing in each. In principle, and observing for the moment solely in economic terms, we must presume that different districts are capable of bargaining their relationships in different ways. Be that as it may, as far as the district is concerned, a point of no return would be if it no longer became viable for single local firms to stay together in a particular economic and social environment after following different directions externally. One or more network-firms might replace them in their previous markets and steal space from many of them indefinitely. After being colonised, a district might thus be abandoned to a destiny of decadence, to the changing circumstances and convenience of a large-scale multinational firm playing and choosing its partners on the world stage.

This picture is an overdramatic one. In some cases, a market may be colonised for exploitation of its cheap labour for elementary manufacturing processes. This may also lead to a drop in economic conditions and wages, especially in the more traditional districts. In other cases and, arguably, increasingly in developed countries, the network-firm's relationship with districts may be based on the advantage of a specialised interfirm division of labour, exploiting the technical and other know-how developed by each firm involved. There are no reasons of principle to believe that a district cannot continue to be a reciprocally favourable environment for many small firms involved in external relations – that is, with more than one network-firm – of this kind. Nor are there reasons of principle to believe that large firms do not have an interest in the persistence of these districts. As for dependence margins, this is a question that has to be worked out. In principle, it is necessary to beware of the simple idea of colonisation, although this may be the reality in many cases, and we must prepare lists of analytical variables capable of supplying typologies of adaptation. Of course, in this perspective we have to expect greater relations than in the past between small firms or districts and large-scale firms with governance functions, and lower internal integration of local systems. But was this not a characteristic of the German or French cases, with respect to the Italian one, anyway?

There is a second side to the question that has to be considered. In its simple forms, a district's firms comprised a system insofar as they were interconnected by market regulated subsupply relations, facilitated and cemented by mutual acquaintance and ease of circulation of information. In this way it was possible to achieve both elasticity on unstable markets and adaptability to differentiated markets. The miracle of mircoelectronics was that it lent small plants a technological growth which permitted them to maintain elasticity. The functional problem that emerged at a certain point was due to the incapability of the combination of simple market and traditional relations to act as a back-up towards modernisation. Relations between small firms then began to be stabilised by appropriate organisational structures for joint ventures and long-term agreements were also tried, as well as consortia, cooperative arrangements and shareholdings. In this way it was possible to accept a reasonable risk for investments that would be profitable in the longer term. Also the tendency towards greater financial concentration and dispersed production could be seen, in a certain sense, as the possible endogenous trend of districts of small firms. Otherwise, however, the common organisation of governance structures and functions and of support to the system as such was an evolutionary tendency of the old autonomous industrial districts. The tendency often relied on the institutional action of politics and government investment. Working in this direction, it is possible to develop districts with a greater capacity to withstand competition from network-firms from an autonomous position, or to enter into contact with them from a position of greater strength.

We are still not well acquainted with these processes. A great deal of empirical research is needed to enable us to put the different modes of reaction to the test of time. However, we do receive confirmation of the point of view whereby it is the mode of integration of the economy in society which is important for understanding local economic systems and the destiny of districts. The mode of integration has assumed new forms: organisation and politics are acquiring importance over the simple free market and community relations. Political action capable of integrating a society which has become more differentiated tends to replace the functions of common cultural roots. Without a sound policy of local infrastructure and back-up services to firms, without efficient local and national administration, and without the capacity of districts to obtain a national support policy in the international framework, local economies of small firms lose out.

Basically, a district may play its cards right if the actors continue to invest economically and socially at district level, and if institutional arrangements facilitate it and make it acceptable to the actors. It is likely, for example, that it is precisely here, rather than in the adaptability of firms, that the main source of weakness of many Italian districts resides. For other districts may apply the more predictable interpretations of economic weakness on markets that tend to remain traditional.

Large industry has dominated the scenario for almost two centuries. It continues to do so today through the network-firm. Over the last few decades small firms have demonstrated a vitality that was totally unexpected. Now life has become harder for them but they still have cards up their sleeves.

The moral of the story

Districts of small firms or, in more general terms, as we established at the beginning, local systems with a diffuse economic base, in which small firms count for a lot, are relatively independent and – at least to a certain extent – capable of strategy, have a future if actors are prepared to invest sufficiently in them; in other words, if adequate complicity is formed between economic and institutional actors.

If we look at the research tradition, we note a certain complicity also on the part of those who have studied small firms – when, for example, in the 1970s, Giacomo Becattini or Sebastiano Brusco suggested that the experiences of diffuse industrialisation were not to be liquidated simply as a residue of the past, nor simply in economic terms. Or when, a few years later, Sabel and Zeitlin spoke about them as possible historical alternatives to mass production. Or, more recently, when Alain Lipietz suggested that, in possible local compromises, environment, quality of life and urban conviviality are in play against regional gigantism and hyper-concentration. All these analyses betray complicity and sympathy. This is, of course, a risky position from which to make analysis; sometimes it has forced errors and perhaps, in some cases, exaggerations of the strength and strategic capacity of small firm systems. It is, however, probably a necessary attitude to the subject if some of the possibilities are not to elude us. No one has ever hidden the fact that small may be and often is – and to some extent may be again – bad. But it is also necessary to remember that some European regions with diffuse economies have been among those in which economic possibilities have been most equally shared among the population, services best organised and local government most participative. We must beware of possible new hybrids; or, to put it a different way, to anyone wishing, theoretically, to sweep under the carpet an attitude of experimental benevolence towards small firms, we may respond that: 'There are more things in heaven and earth...than are dreamt of in your philosophy.'

1

INDUSTRIAL POLICY AND SMALL-FIRM COOPERATION IN BADEN-WÜRTTEMBERG

KLAUS SEMLINGER

Introduction: industrial districts revisited

After a period of enthusiastic appreciation, scepticism is growing with regard to the prospects for prosperity of small firms and the value of 'industrial districts' as a general model for regional policy. It is becoming more and more apparent that such an approach of 'cooperative endogenous development' requires growing investments of capital, research and qualification which are likely to overtax the capabilities of small firms, and it is still uncertain whether the underlying concept of supply (i.e. the supply of diversified custom-made quality products) will find a correspondingly growing demand.

Nevertheless, these objections and caveats do not deny the possibility (or even necessity) of regional development based on (resident) small firms. Baden-Württemberg, which is a popular example among the international collection of productive regional networks, quite impressively demonstrates how – by means of interfirm cooperation – small firms can maintain their competitive stance against big business, and how – in the same way – a region can develop its innovative potential. Since 1991, however, the Baden-Württemberg economy has lost its prosperous dynamics and the region now seems to suffer from what was formerly its asset (i.e. its concentration on 'flexible specialisation' and 'diversified quality production').

Thus, to reconsider the opportunities and prerequisites of a successful cooperative development of regional small-firm economies it is worth retelling the story of Baden-Württemberg. I will start with some statistics about its economy and then describe briefly the specific 'pan-enterprise' approach of industrial policy traditionally applied in Baden-Württemberg, some special features of its institutional infrastructure and some experiences with regard to small-firm cooperation. The concluding remarks will point to some policy conclusions of a more general kind.

A short portrait of the Baden-Württemberg economy

Baden-Württemberg accounts for 16.5 per cent of the West German gross domestic product.[1] During the 1980s the growth rates of its economy were continuously higher than those of the West German economy as a whole. However, with regard to economic growth, other German states – Bavaria and Hesse – have been even more successful, and in regard to productivity, Bavaria has made greater headway, while Hesse is quite impressively in the lead.

Although the region has joined the general trend toward a 'service economy', manufacturing has retained a far above average share of employment and value added (47.2 per cent and 47.3 per cent respectively compared to 40.6 per cent and 40.1 per cent for the FRG average). Today Baden-Württemberg is a more industrialised state than even North Rhine-Westphalia. But it is not manufacturing in general which has found its place in Baden-Württemberg: with 66 per cent of employment and 61 per cent of sales it is capital goods production which clearly dominates its manufacturing industry (FRG: 55 per cent and 48 per cent). A closer look reveals that mechanical engineering, automobile production and electrical engineering form the backbone of the regional economy. More than 90 per cent of the increase in general employment in manufacturing during the last 40 years derives from these three industries, which nowadays account for about half of the employment in manufacturing.

Nevertheless, the assessment of this success has to take into account that these industries have also boomed elsewhere. According to a rough calculation, the increase of employment in Baden-Württemberg over the last forty years in electrical engineering has not been higher than in Germany as a whole; only in machine building was the increase about one third higher than the average and the automobile industry grew some 40 per cent more. Thus, part of the region's success derives from the generally growing importance of its dominant industries, which is not to deny that many of its (world-famous) enterprises have markedly contributed to the prosperous development of their kind.

Despite this somewhat different reading of its story of success, Baden-Württemberg legitimately has the reputation of a 'high-tech economy'. Its industrial profile is determined not only by automobile, machine and electrical goods production, but also by a special emphasis on advanced products and state-of-the-art engineering for the upper segments of these markets. The main source for this competence is human skills. Compared with the national average the manufacturing industry in Baden-Württemberg employs considerably more highly qualified labour (i.e. natural scientists and engineers). At the same time, however, there is a below average share of skilled labour (*Facharbeiter*) among blue-collar workers. Put together, the Baden-Württemberg economy features a somewhat 'dualized' employment structure with regard to qualification.

In addition, the image of Baden-Württemberg as an SME economy has to be qualified (Schmitz, 1992). In fact, the region shows an over-proportional share of craft establishments and employees in the craft sector (1990: 18.3 per cent and 17.3 per cent respectively) and 96.5 per cent of its enterprises in manufacturing industry have fewer than 100 employees. However, this corresponds to the average German pattern. Measured by their share of employment, small firms (fewer than 100 employees) are less important and large-companies (1000 and more employees) are more dominant in Baden-Württemberg than for the average of all West German states. Even North Rhine-Westfalia, which is commonly considered to be dominated by industrial dinosaurs, looks more like an SME economy than the supposed homeland of the '*Mittelstand*'.[2]

Furthermore, economic activity is fairly concentrated in the greater Stuttgart area, accounting for 25 per cent of the region's population and 10 per cent of its space, the area is responsible for more than 30 per cent of gross value added and hosts about 31 per cent of the jobs in manufacturing and even 40 per cent of the territory's R&D personnel in private enterprises. With regard to the dominant industries, the importance of the area is even more significant. Measured by its share of sales, Stuttgart and the surrounding area account for 60 per cent in the automobile industry, 47 per cent in electrical/electronic goods production and 33 per cent in mechanical engineering. In this area, large firms provide more than half of the jobs in manufacturing. Taking into account the many subsidiaries of these large firms outside the area, it turns out that more than half of all industrial employees in Baden-Württemberg find their headquarters here.

In correspondence with its economic success, Baden-Württemberg has provided an increasing number of people with gainful employment. Accordingly, the region's labour force (and population) has grown in absolute numbers and relative weight. Since 1990, however, the increase in employment in Baden-Württemberg has been lower than the German average and the increase in GDP no longer exceeds the national average. In fact, it seems that the current economic crisis has hit Baden-Württemberg worse than West Germany as a whole; although its unemployment rate is still below that of other German states, in 1992 it jumped by about 50 per cent and had increased to 6 per cent in April 1993.

Obviously, the region suffers from some specific problems which add to the pressure of generally declining demand and increased international competition (Cooke and Morgan, 1993). Most importantly, since it affects the specific profile of manufacturing in Baden-Württemberg price competition has reached high-end markets. Accordingly, what had been a competitive advantage is threatening to turn into a handicap. As previously argued, manufacturing in Baden-Württemberg is based on technological competence, which enables its leading firms to specialise in highly sophisticated products and those specifically designed to the individual needs of single clients. Today, many customers cannot or will not afford the high costs of this kind of 'diversified quality production' and 'flexible specialisation', – especially because there is an increasing number of (international) suppliers offering (almost) equivalent products at (reasonable) lower prices. Correspondingly, what once was appreciated as a 'state-of-the-art' product is now considered 'over-engineered'. Thus, what is necessary is not 'just' further advancements in R&D and product development, an accelerated rationalisation of production processes and a reorganisation of industrial structure, but a reorientation in product philosophy, market strategy and in the way technological competence is applied.

Industrial policy, institutional infrastructure and inter-firm cooperation in Baden-Württemberg

Although it is far from being irrefutable that the clue to the economic development of the region is to be found in its institutional framework and the industrial policy applied rather than in the growth of 'sunrise industries' (Schmitz, 1992), there is reason to believe that the latter would not have occurred (here in the region and as prosperously as it has been) completely independent of the region's specific institutional background. Thus, to understand the economic success of Baden-Württemberg in the past and to estimate its future prospects, a closer look at its institutional infrastructure is necessary.[3]

Industrial policy by pan-enterprise institutional support

Industry in Baden-Württemberg has its roots in a system of commercial cottage industry and artisan production, which from the outset was forced to lean on its human resources (i.e. on work attitude and qualification). Thus, quite early in its history it had to find its place in competitive niches (i.e. to specialise in processing industries with a diversity of quality and precision products).

Public policy has supported this path of development, employing a 'synthesis approach of mercantilism and economic liberalism' (Maier, 1987: 26), designed to improve the ability of self-help for private economic initiatives. With this aim, apart from developing a regional system of local loan and savings banks (starting in 1818), a Central Bureau of Trade and Commerce was set up as a governmental agency for in-kind promotion of private business as early as 1848. Run by Ferdinand Steinbeis, who became head of the bureau in 1855, this agency carried out a multitude of support programmes such as hiring foreign experts to work as travelling teachers, exhibiting advanced foreign technology in order to stimulate its adoption and reproduction, endowing selected artisans with advanced machinery from abroad, organising local trade exhibitions and encouraging resident firms to participate in international fairs. In addition, Steinbeis succeeded in transforming the dispersed early attempts of vocational schooling into a comprehensive system of vocational education and further training.

Thus, when worldwide demand for automobiles, machine tools and electric/electronic devices increased, these industries in

Baden-Württemberg were well equipped with creative firms and a well-educated labour force.[4] Moreover, there emerged a system of interfirm relationships through which many firms developed their unique profile of competence and had the opportunity to interact with other specialised partners. While some firms have turned to (qualified) mass production and have become large (international) companies, many others remained small, serving their own (world) market niche or working as a supplier to the big brand names. This specific organisation of industry proved to be highly competitive, especially with regard to the more sophisticated market segments which call for flexible customised production.

Since World War II public policy has continued to promote this development by in-cash as well as by in-kind support. Apart from public grants, financial help has mainly been provided by subsidised loans and guarantees either through the Landeskreditbank (Regional Loans Bank) or the Bürgschaftsbank (Security Bank Baden-Württemberg). On the other hand, in-kind support, at least up to the early 1980s, has mainly been supplied by the Landesgewerbeamt (Regional Trade Bureau), which was set up as early as 1952, the year when Baden-Württemberg was founded as a unified state of the Federal Republic of Germany. The support it offers, primarily to small and medium-sized firms, consists of consulting services, the operation of information centres (including databank facilities), facilitation of interfirm cooperation (see pp. 25–26), and – not least – the promotion of further training. In fact, one of the outstanding institutional successes of the Bureau has been the stimulation of cooperation among the different institutions engaged in further training, which is unique in Germany. As early as 1968 – on an initiative of the Bureau – these institutions joined together into fifty-nine Committees for Further Training at local level collectively to promote the issue, advertise their programmes, and estimate (future) training needs.

However, the economic recessions of the 1970s and early 1980s called for structural change in Baden-Württemberg, as elsewhere. In response, as in other German states, the regional government modernised its industrial policy, gave more emphasis to technological development and innovation and enlarged its support programmes for small and medium-sized firms. For example, new subsidy schemes were created to help start-ups of technology-oriented new firms and a special Venture Capital Fund (*Mittelständische Beteiligungsgesellschaft*) was founded as a publicly subsidised, private self-help institution.

However financial aid to individual firms has remained of comparatively minor importance. Instead, following its long tradition, the regional government further developed its (in-kind) pan-enterprise support measures.[5] It is impossible to enumerate all the different activities and programmes which are initiated or affected by this endeavour. Therefore, the following will concentrate on two fields of major importance, namely vocational training and technological development.

To support apprenticeship training and further training, the regional government spent about DM 150 million between 1986–9 to help the start-up or modernisation and work of Joint Training Centres and of the above-mentioned Committees for Further Training.[6] In addition, in 1983 a Regional Committee for Further Training was set up, which since then has been jointly developing concepts for this part of vocational education and, thus, providing some guidance to compensate for a gap in public vocational regulation, which in Germany primarily refers to apprenticeship education of young people.

Furthermore, there is another institution in vocational education which was specific to Baden-Württemberg and has only recently been imitated elsewhere, the Berufsakademie Baden-Württemberg (Vocational Academy). Going back to an initiative of some well-known large regional companies, this Academy was founded in 1974. The idea is to offer vocational education (primarily in economics and engineering) to young people who have passed the upper secondary school examination (*Abitur*), thus being entitled to go to university but preferring a shorter, more practical training programme. Like regular apprenticeship training, education is divided into schooling at the Academy and practical training at the firm to which the trainee is affiliated by contract. During the 1970s the Academy was enlarged to eight sites. In the school year 1990–91, 11,000 students were enrolled; almost 20 per cent came from enterprises outside Baden-Württemberg.[7]

Additionally, industrial policy has become even more technology oriented than it had already been from the start (see Bernschneider *et al.*, 1991; Hofmann, 1991): Apart from new subsidy schemes, as in other regions, Baden-Württernberg has set up (ten) Technology Centres in proximity to a university which are to provide (subsidised) space and services for young high-technology firms. Additionally, the scientific infrastructure, already quite well developed, was further improved by the foundation of at least nine new industry-related research institutes and an Academy for

Technology Assessment. Today, Baden-Württemberg hosts 9 universities, 6 teacher training colleges, 7 art colleges, 38 polytechnics (*Fachhochschulen*), 14 Max Planck Institutes, 14 Fraunhofer Institutes, 3 FRG Research Centres, 10 AIF industrial research institutes,[8] and some dozen other non-university research institutes.

Technology transfer got a further push in 1982, when a Commissioner for Technology Transfer was appointed to the Minister President. In 1983 this commissioner also became head of the Steinbeis Foundation, which is a private organisation supervised by a board consisting of representatives from private business, the scientific community, political parties, regional ministries and the Landeskreditbank, and which at that time, had taken over the responsibility for technology transfer from the Landesgewerbeamt. Since then, the Foundation has set up a new network of Technology Transfer Centres, which are mainly attached to the regional polytechnics and are autonomously run by professors of the respective schools. The network itself, in turn, functions more or less like a non-profit franchise system with the Foundation restricting itself to some overhead services. In contrast to technology transfer centres elsewhere in Germany, the Steinbeis Transfer Centres are not just brokering agencies, but help directly with R&D support.

In building up this network – within eight years – Baden-Württemberg has filled a gap in the German institutional R&D landscape with regard to the needs of SMEs. As elsewhere, there are the institutes of the Max Planck Society (MPG) and the universities, both of which work mainly on basic research or in cooperation with big companies. On the other hand, the institutes of the Fraunhofer Society (FhG) are engaged in (advanced) applied research but also usually in cooperation with large firms. Only the research groups of the AIF provide applied research for small and medium-sized firms, but not on individual request. Nowadays, with about 120 Steinbeis Transfer Centres in 29 towns, small firms in Baden-Württemberg have an address to contact if they need individual R&D support.

Finally, worth mentioning is the organizational reform of industrial policy, which aimed mainly at streamlining the administrative system and centralization of strategic decision-making (Bernschneider *et al.* 1991, Hofmann 1991). Industrial policy was taken up as a priority issue by the Minister President. The responsibility for technology promotion was concentrated at the Ministry of Economics and the Commissioner for Technology Transfer, while the implementation of respective programmes with regard to the individual enterprise was assigned to the publicly owned yet privately organized Landeskreditbank and the Steinbeis Foundation. In the end, this reform resulted in some reduction of parliamentary control and enabled central agencies to overrule the lower echelons of public administration and local politics. While this reorganisation increased the flexibility of industrial policy and put administrative units under competitive pressure, part of the enlarged room for manoeuvre and power of discretion was handed over to the addressees (i.e. to the firms or the (local) organizations of business interests), which are supposed to know best where to develop, how to proceed and what help to needed.

To sum up, during the 1980s the modernisation of industrial policy in Baden-Württemberg led to further amendments to an already advanced institutional infrastructure of pan-enterprise support. Special emphasis was given to the improvement of knowledge and (mutual) information. In addition, strategic decision-making was more centralised while implementation became more decentralised. Although the government explicitly confessed to an active industrial policy, it also maintained the prevailing maxim that public support of private business should restrict itself to improving the ability for self-help. Yet all these amendments obviously could not prevent regional industry from getting trapped by the success of flexible specialisation when markets changed at the beginning of the 1990s, and they have been unable to meet increasing pressure for enlarged and improved inter-firm and inter-organizational cooperation.

Cooperation among small firms as a public-private joint venture

Cooperation is one of the prerequisites of industrial district development. Unlike large industry, however, small firms still have their subjective reservations and objective difficulties with cooperative action (see Semlinger 1991a). In Germany there are well-developed networks of institutionalised cooperation and business organisation, which provide a good basis for collaborative interaction. Yet this is only partially true for small firms because:

1. As a rule small business is significantly less well organized in the voluntary associations of private business.
2. The work of these associations depends on voluntary contribu-

tions from their member firms, which, in turn, are normally quite restricted if these firms are small.

3. In associations which can count on the support of large member firms, the interests of small firms often get lost – in part because in this case the work on the panels and committees is carried out by delegates of the bigger companies.

There is no evidence that the situation in Baden-Württemberg is very different. For example, the Employer's Association of the Metal Industry (Gesamtmetall), which covers most of the manufacturing sector, has two regional chapters in Baden-Württemberg, one for the north, including the greater Stuttgart area, and a smaller one for the south. The northern branch (North Württemberg/North Baden) has 912 member firms with a total of about 545,000 employees (1989). About 10 per cent of the member firms have more than 1,000 employees, which is far above their proportional share of industrial enterprises. Bearing in mind that the automobile industry alone counts for 34 per cent of the member firms' employment, one can estimate the influence a few large companies such as Daimler-Benz and Bosch have in the politics and on the policy of the association.[9]

In addition, some qualifications have to be made concerning the image of the Baden-Württemberg economy as a dense network of direct inter-firm cooperation. First, in contrast to the close cooperation with their customers, for which German machine-building firms are famous (vertical cooperation), horizontal cooperation in this industry has traditionally been only of minor significance and only recently – since the industry has faced severe problems – have corresponding ideas have received some attention. This situation also applies in Baden-Württemberg. Second, the machine tool industry and by far the most important automobile manufacturer in the region are well known for their high reliance on in-house production.[10] Today, when many companies refer increasingly to 'outsourcing', they are looking for new sources not just among regional suppliers but outside the region and even abroad. Finally, although in general enlarged and intensified buyer-supplier relationships are labelled as 'cooperation', it should be acknowledged that much of what happens here looks rather like henchmanship and is fairly different from a consensual and balanced partnership (Semlinger 1991a, 1993).

On the other hand, in Baden-Württemberg the promotion of

inter-firm cooperation among small firms has been made a policy issue since the early 1970s. Towards this end, the Landesgewerbeamt is administering a programme, which provides subsidies for consulting and brokerage services to help cooperation get started and become organized, for travelling expenses in connection with network meetings, and for up to 50 per cent of the costs incurred by the development of joint projects. However, the impact of this in-cash support should not be overstated. What seems to be more important is the personal assistance (i.e. the in-kind support for cooperative activities). In this way, the Landesgewerbeamt was able to stimulate about 200 inter-firm networks. Not every initiative is still functioning, but others are flourishing and have stimulated imitation even outside Baden-Württemberg. This applies, for example, to one of the oldest and most ambitious examples of small firm cooperation in Baden-Württemberg, the Committee of Suppliers Baden Württemberg (AKZ).

This Committee, organised as a loosely coupled network of independent firms, was set up in 1972 when a small business entrepreneur approached the Landesgewerbeamt to complain about the lack of opportunities for small firms to participate in industrial fairs. In line with its cooperative approach, the Landesgewerbeamt offered help by organising a meeting for firms with similar problems. Starting as a group of about 12, its membership grew in the first year to 23 enterprises from all over Baden-Württemberg, with a total of 725 employees. Afterwards there was some fluctuation but basically no increase in the number of member firms. Today, the group consists of 26 enterprises, most of which engage in electrical and mechanical engineering, tool-making and/or other fields of precision metal working. The total employment of the member firms increased to about 2,000 employees and total sales reached DM 320 million by 1990.

However, in order to become the stable and active network it is today, the circle had to overcome a number of difficulties. As reported at the beginning, there was a rather confused debate about the perspectives of the group and 'too much discussion' about the goals it should aim for. The proposal (from the head of the Landesgewerbeamt) to organise a joint exhibition at the Hannover Industry fair, finally structured the debate. This idea was realised in 1974 and led to the development of a special 'Suppliers market', which since then has become a regular part of the world's largest industrial fair.

In the years that followed, the Committee enlarged its scope of cooperation. However, as reported by its first chairman, who was the driving force and coordinator of the group until 1989, this did not happen without some friction. At first there was a lot of scepticism and a number of firms rejected close cooperation, since member firms at least partially competed for the same customers or even for the same jobs. Accordingly, it required continuous stimulation, persuasion and even arbitration to keep the initiative alive and developing work, which, according to an outsider, occupied the attention of the chairman to such an extent that at times he was neglecting his own business. Today, the member firms meet about ten times a year to exchange information and experiences or to listen to an invited expert. In addition, they organize mutual plant visits and are engaged in further collective marketing activities (sometimes even in joint bidding).

In 1992 regional government further enlarged its efforts to promote inter-firm and inter-institutional cooperation. At the same time, a broader approach of tripartite collaboration was introduced into the formation of industrial policy (i.e. the Economics Ministry invited representatives of private enterprises, business organisations and trade unions to agree on collective action with regard to the improvement of vocational qualification and the modernisation of industry).

Between October 1992 and April 1993 three 'summit meetings' were organised for the automobile (suppliers), the machine-building and the textile and garment industries of the region. Each meeting produced a common understanding of preferred strategic options for the respective industry and concluded in a number of concrete proposals. As a result, firms are invited to join in collective projects for the development and application of new production and organisation techniques, new products and the improvement of interaction among firms (especially with regard to simultaneous engineering, synchronized production and modern quality management). These projects will be supported by the scientific infrastructure of the region and subsidised by the Economics Ministry.

In addition, the Steinbeis Foundation obtained an additional fund (DM 4.5 million for a period of three years) to set up a consulting and brokerage service especially for small and medium-sized firms. The chambers of commerce and the different business organisations promised to enlarge their corresponding services. In a new 'productivity pact' the metal workers union and the respective employers associations have agreed on a cooperative attempt to promote the implementation of reforms in the organisation of work at the enterprise level (especially with regard to lean management and the extension of flexible working-time schemes and group work). Finally, in February 1993, the Minister President convened a Committee, 'Economy 2000', consisting of high-level scientists and business representatives to elaborate on the perspectives of new technological fields which promise to provide basic innovations to push forward mature industries or to open up completely new industrial alternatives.

Conclusion: a cooperative approach to industrial policy

Much of the image of Baden-Württemberg as an SME economy flourishing by inter-firm cooperation due to a successful industrial policy has to be revised. Nevertheless, even if its prosperity primarily derives from its fortune in being home to some of the most important modern growth industries, this is not just by chance. Rather, there is good reason to believe that localisation and development of these industries – in this particular region with its past prosperity – was effectively stimulated and supported by its specific institutional background. Thus, although it would be misleading to claim that the ultimate base of the economic success of Baden-Württemberg lies in its institutional infrastructure and industrial policy, it has to be acknowledged that they have facilitated the development of the economy in general and of its small firms in particular.

It took more than one hundred years before Baden-Württemberg could experience its economic breakthrough – a time in which policy and economy have mutually influenced each other to form the specific socioeconomic profile of the region, namely that of an institutionally rich 'engineering economy' (Cooke and Morgan 1993). In this process of reciprocal interaction, policy and the emerging institutions have promoted some options (i.e. those of a skill-intensive economy) and hampered others (i.e. especially those of low-wage cost competition). In the end, this led to the regional economy becoming one of the prototypes for 'flexible specialisation' and 'diversified quality production'.

'Flexible specialisation' and 'diversified quality production', however, call for a more decentralised yet integrated organisation of production (Semlinger, 1993). The more the different tasks of production have to be divided between independent firms to improve efficiency by specialisation and flexibility by loose coupling, the more need there is for a pattern of coordination which is less static than 'hierarchy' and more stable than 'market'. What is necessary is 'negotiated flexibility' (Streeck, 1991) and 'coordinated specialization' (Herrigel, 1990); otherwise a growing division of labour would just lead to increasing individual risks and flexibility would turn into mere turbulence.

In Baden-Württemberg this coordination was, for a long time, mainly achieved within conventional (vertical) buyer-supplier-relationships and by the guidance provided by the different organisations of private business. During recent years, when the dominant industries of the region have matured and price competition has also reached high-end markets, this coordination has become insufficient. Many companies which are world famous for their state-of-the-art engineering have reacted to these new challenges and try to reduce costs by making moves down market and increasing standardisation in their products – as well as by quitting collective agreements on wages or cutting back voluntary payments. In addition, the large dominant companies of the automobile industry not only increasingly resorted to outsourcing but also put their subcontractors under intensified pressure. Partially in reaction to this development, other firms are looking for more direct (horizontal) cooperation with companies of their own kind.

However, even now many small firms are reluctant to cooperate. Accordingly – and not only in Baden-Württemberg – the promotion of horizontal inter-firm cooperation among small firms has to become a priority issue of industrial policy, as such initiatives are evidently in need of personal assistance and institutional support in order to get started, oriented and organised. This is not to say that industrial policy has to provide ready-made answers to the problems of the single firm or to the difficulties of cooperative interaction, nor does it have to prescribe ready-made blueprints for the economic development of a whole region. Rather its main tasks are to organize time and provoke attention in enterprise decision-making to enable or enforce (continuous) reconsideration of standard practices and new opportunities and to provide additional information to overcome the propensity for 'simple-minded search'. In the end, industrial policy, too, should apply a more 'cooperative approach' (Semlinger, 1991 a, b), which means substituting direct normative or in-cash interventions with a more indirect normative or in-kind context regulation of the decision-making processes of its addressees by 'framing' their set of decision opportunities and their perception of these opportunities.

In Baden-Württemberg this approach to industrial policy already has some tradition and the new initiatives serve to develop further measures which carry on this tradition. By improving public information services, promoting better interaction between private business and the public R&D infrastructure and in negotiating mutual collaboration, regional government actively supports the going adjustment processes and tries to keep them on track in order to safeguard the achieved standards of a 'high road to development'.

Notes

1. Here, and in the following, every comparison to an FRG standard or average refers to the Federal Republic of Germany excluding the states of the former German Democratic Republic.
2. According to census data (1987) the employment shares of small firms and big firms respectively are: Baden-Württemberg 26.4 per cent and 42.1 per cent, North Rhine-Westphalia 30.5 per cent and 37.5 per cent, national average 30.1 per cent and 40.5 per cent.
3. For the following see Maier (1987); Cooke and Morgan 1990; Herrigel (1990); Bechtle et al. (1992); Pyke (1992); Schmitz (1992).
4. Note, however, that the textile industry was the dominant industry even in 1952.
5. Between 1986 and 1989 the regional government supplied SMEs with DM 3.716 million in loans, DM 1.273 million in securities and DM 249 million in grants. In total, grants and (interest) costs for loans and securities (i.e. expenditure for in-cash support to individual firms) amounted to DM 562.7 million, while pan-enterprise (in-kind) support measures amounted to DM 561 million.
6. In 1989 there were about 80 Joint Training Centres with about 7,700 training places; between the years 1986–9 these centres alone accounted for more than 27,000 courses with 356,000 participants.
7. However, due to the fact that schooling at the Academy is strictly bound to the practical needs of private enterprises, the diplomas of the Academy lack general public recognition.

8. The AIF (Association of Industrial Research Groups), founded in 1954 on a joint initiative of the Federal Ministry of Economics and the Federal Association of German Industry (BDI), is explicitly supposed to encourage collective research among SMEs. 'Collective research' in this context is defined as projects supported by the majority of firms of a specific industry without exclusion of any competitor who would like to join and with the obligation openly to publish all results.

9. At the same time, North Württemberg/North–Baden is the region with the most powerful chapter of the Trade Union of Metalworkers (IG Metall), which in turn is the biggest trade union in Germany (2.7 million members in 1989). Accordingly, and because its dominant industries/enterprises belonged to the most prosperous parts of German industry, this region has been the preferred battleground for collective bargaining. Here, the union achieved preferential agreements on wages, working hours, dismissal protection and participation in human resource management (Cooke and Morgan 1990; Schmitz 1992; Bechtle *et al.* 1992). Many small firm employers, however, are complaining about these compromises. Especially small suppliers feel squeezed, seeing themselves trapped between the pressure big customers put on their prices and the cost push from the wage increases the employer's association have agreed upon.

10. In 1989 large machine-building companies (in Germany) had an average share of in-house production of 56 per cent, for medium-sized companies (1,000–4,000 employees) the figure was 49 per cent and for smaller enterprises 59 per cent. In contrast, the average share of in-house production of German car manufacturers was 35 per cent (in 1987), that of Daimler-Benz, however, was 46 per cent.

2

A TALE OF TWO DISTRICTS: WORK AND POLITICS IN THE THIRD ITALY*

CARLO TRIGILIA

The development of small firms can be seen as one of the most significant aspects of the process of adjustment to the economic and social tensions of the 1970s in Italy. The term 'adjustment' emphasises that this process was largely unplanned, though it was influenced by political decisions or, more frequently, non-decisions. In the absence of effective long-term economic policies at the central level, the growth of small firms has, in fact, been based on certain economic, social and political resources which were widely available in some local areas. These allowed smaller productive units to seize the opportunities for development which were opened up by changes in technology, in the organisation of work and in market structures.

The regions in which small firms predominate – Emilia, Tuscany, Umbria, the Marches, Veneto, Trentino and Friuli – are located principally in the centre and north-east of the country. The phenomenon is also to be found in the north-west, where the large firms undergoing restructuring and the large metropolitan areas are concentrated, and in the south, where the major problems remain those associated with underdevelopment. The regions of the so-called 'Third Italy' are, therefore, characterised by the marked predominance of small firms. The 'traditional' sectors of industry – textiles, clothing, shoes and furniture – predominate,

* A slightly different version of this text, which we are grateful to have been given permission to publish, appeared in F. Dyke, G. Becattini and W. Sengenberger, *Industrial Districts and Interfirm Cooperation in Italy*, International Institute for Labour Studies, Geneva, 1990.

but there is also a significant development of 'modern' sectors, particularly the machine tool industry. Small firms tend to be found clustered together in 'industrial districts' (Becattini, 1987). They form integrated territorial systems with strong sectoral specialization. These districts usually coincide with small urban areas and consist of one or more communities.

Numerous studies clearly indicated that there was a relationship between this form of development and the social context in which it occurred. Diffuse industrialisation was supported by a complex institutional structure which consisted not only of social components, such as the extended family and the local community, but also of specific political components which influenced industrial relations and the local governments' activities. The regions which are most typical of small-firm development (as with similar areas in Piedmont and Lombardy) have been characterised by the existence of specific subcultures, that is by the predominance of a particular political tradition, whose origins usually go back to the beginnings of the century, and a complex of institutions (parties, interest groups, cultural and welfare structures) which derive from the same politico-ideological matrix. The central regions, which were originally Socialist in orientation, became Communist strongholds after World War II, while there was a deeply-rooted Catholic subculture in the regions of the north-east.

In the perspective of economic sociology, when a great number of institutional factors seem to be at work in a process of development, detailed case studies of representative experiences can be useful. The first part of this chapter presents the story of two typical small-firm districts. In the following sections more general aspects of the relationship between work and politics are discussed. It is important to take into account that the picture refers to small-firm Italy in the 1970s and early 1980s. The situation has significantly changed in the ensuing period, especially in two aspects that are worth mentioning.

First, the regions of the Third Italy seem to have diverged during recent years in their path of development. Some of them, such as Veneto and Emilia have had the highest rate of development among the Italian regions, while other small-firm areas have not been able to keep pace. It is likely that sector specialisation has influenced that outcome. However, the research programme on which this chapter is based[1] already stressed that the future of small-firm regions would be more dependent on their ability to integrate the role of traditional cultural and social resources with a higher degree of industrial organisation and with new public policies more adequate to the new challenges. New research on these aspects could probably help to explain the emerging differences in the adjustment of small-firm regions.

Second, in recent years there has been a decline in traditional political subcultures. Especially the 'white' (Catholic) areas have been characterised by the impressive growth of the Lega, a new political movement which calls for political and fiscal decentralisation and which is opposed to the traditional parties. The left-wing tradition of the 'red' areas seems to be more resistant to the Lega's attack, although a decline of the traditional subculture is clearly visible, even in the central regions. Again, new research is necessary to understand the effects of these political changes on the problems of modernisation of the small-firm regions.

A tale of two districts

In the early 1980s the areas of Valdelsa in Tuscany and Bassano in Veneto were two typical small firm districts. The former lies across the border of the provinces of Florence and Siena. The latter is in the northern part of the province of Vicenza. Each of the two districts had an overall population of less than 100,000 in 1981. Their largest centres, Poggibonsi and Bassano, accounted for 26,000 and 38,000 people respectively. A diffuse type of settlement is a long-standing feature of these areas that can be traced back to the period of the Italian city-states. The rural population became scattered in the countryside as a consequence of the prevailing production relations: sharecropping in Valdelsa, very small peasant property and sharecropping in the area of Bassano.

In both cases, the economy was mainly agricultural until after World War II, but there are local traditions of commerce and handicraft, and some early industrialisation was brought about by external initiatives. Around Bassano, ceramics and woodwork are local traditions. A flourishing wool industry died out a the end of the eighteenth century. The art of printing also went into crisis during the nineteenth century, after a period of strong growth; but some traces of it remain. In the case of Valdelsa, the industries of paper and glass, and the activities of weaving and spinning, which were practised by sharecropping families, were of early significance; woodwork arrived later.

After World War II growth was extremely fast in both cases. In 1951 agriculture was still an important sector, accounting for 40 per cent of employees in the area of Bassano, and for 60 per cent in Valdelsa. Between 1951 and 1981 manufacturing industry grew by about 250 per cent in Valdelsa and 160 per cent in the already more advanced Bassano area.

In both cases the prevailing sectors in the 1980s were the 'traditional' ones: in Valdelsa, furniture, glass and, to a lesser extent, clothing and shoemaking are significant; in Bassano, shoemaking is more important while furniture and ceramics are also of note. But a mechanical engineering branch of some importance exists in both districts and is growing, organised in small and medium-sized firms. Small production units clearly prevail in both areas (the average size of units of production is 9.3 employees in Valdelsa and 9.5 in Bassano).

Source of entrepreneurship

Between half and two-thirds of the firms – both industrial and artisanal – were set up after 1960. Management in more than 60 per cent of firms in the two areas is composed of family members and/or relatives, and the proportion of managers and white-collar workers in relation to total employees is not more than 15 per cent in either case. These are typical features of diffuse specialisation. Also typical is that only 24 per cent of industrial entrepreneurs (that is, in firms with more than 10 employees) and artisans (that is, in firms with less than 10 employees) interviewed in the Bassano area and only 22 per cent in the Valdelsa area said that they have a father of the same professional status. The vast majority are therefore first generation entrepreneurs, who receive assistance from family members and relatives. About 50 per cent of them, both in Bassano and Valdelsa have had past experience as waged workers.

Our research allows for an evaluation to be made of the relative contribution of the town and the countryside to the formation of entrepreneurs. In this respect, a direct relationship between a past experience of sharecropping or peasant farming, and small firm entrepreneurship has often been assumed. But this hypothesis seems to require some qualification. Most industrial entrepreneurs have urban roots: more than two-thirds of their fathers – both in Bassano and in Valdelsa – are or were in urban trades. The peasant mould is, relatively speaking, more widespread in the case of artisans; about half the artisans in Valdelsa and 40 per cent in Bassano have, or had, a father employed in agriculture as a sharecropper or peasant farmer. The overall greater contribution to the formation of entrepreneurship – especially of the most strategic industrial sort – has come, therefore, from the traditions of manufacture and commerce existing in the small central and north-eastern towns. Even in the case of the formation of artisanship, where the countryside has made a greater contribution, people with fathers in agriculture would usually have intermediate experience as waged workers in small firms before setting up their own businesses.

Political cultures

While the two districts have very similar socio-economic structures, politically they are very different. This emerges clearly in the vote for the Christian Democratic Party and for the Communist Party in the two areas. Both Valdelsa and the area of Bassano are zones of ancient subcultural settlement. The Socialist movement in Valdelsa and the Catholic movement in Bassano developed and settled in the two areas at the end of the last century.

In Bassano, Catholic identity has roots which go far back into the past; but it was especially between the end of the nineteenth and the first decades of the twentieth century that a network of secular institutions linked with the Church developed alongside the strictly religious ones. In 1909 a Catholic deputy was elected for the first time, and this result was to be confirmed in the next elections in 1913. The extension of suffrage and the beginning of full participation of the Catholics in political life brought about a clear superiority in the polls. The Partito Popolaré (the Catholic party) won the elections held after the war, in 1919 and 1921, acquiring 55 per cent of the votes. After the Fascist period, the historical traditions reasserted themselves in the elections of 1946; the DC (the Christian Democratic Party), which took the place of the Partito Popolaré, gained more than 50 per cent of the vote in Bassano.

The subculture in the Valdelsa area also goes far back in time. The social changes which occurred in the last decades of the nineteenth century with a worsening situation for sharecropping agriculture and a growth of urban centres, laid the conditions for a penetration of Socialist ideas. These were supported, in particular, by the formation of the first nuclei of a working class, and by the existence of social strata of urban, artisan commercial, and industrial lower middle classes, which were under the influence of democratic and liberal opinion. In 1897, the Socialists achieved a majority of votes in the local elections of the Colle Val d'Elsa, which became the first Socialist municipality in Tuscany. The political experience of a 'Municipal Socialism' in the first decades of the twentieth century left a deep mark on local self-identity which Fascism did not manage to erase and which the Resistenza brought back to light. It was indeed through the activity of the Resistenza against Nazism and Fascism that the Communist party acquired a dominant role; this was to be further developed after the war during the struggles of the sharecroppers. In such a way the PCI (Communist Party) ended up as the heir to most of the preceding Socialist political experience.

Family and community institutional context

At the beginning of the 1950s the majority of the population in the areas was made up of agricultural labourers, mainly self-employed, small peasants and sharecroppers. By the 1980s, however, small-firm industrial workers had come to make up the largest social group. They appeared to be young, of local origin, and to a large extent of the first generation.

Despite the new preponderance of industrial workers, the districts display a number of features that contribute to a particularly low degree of proletarianisation. Within the small units of production the way labour is organised inhibits strong class differentiation. Both small entrepreneurs and the members of their families participate directly in the running of the firms (we have already observed that the number of white-collar workers and managers is very small). This leads to direct and personal contact with the workers.

Of further significance are the high expectations of social mobility across socio-economic statuses. While only 20 per cent of workers believed, at the time the research was carried out, that they had concrete possibilities of setting up their own businesses within the next few years (particularly in the tertiary sector), 70 per cent of them held this as an aspiration. We should not, therefore, underestimate the importance that mobility has in maintaining the existence of a social and cultural continuum between workers, artisans, and small entrepreneurs, and in avoiding the erection of rigid class barriers.

This tendency is then strengthened by the fact that uprooting from the community is very limited. Contact with an agricultural background is maintained. This is especially the case in Bassano, probably partly because of the greater historical importance of small peasant property there. Hence, while only 22 per cent of workers in Valdelsa were found to live in isolated houses or cottages, the level went up to 66 per cent for those in Bassano. The latter were also found to more frequently have kitchen gardens and to raise poultry. In any case, most workers owned their home.

The gradual move from agriculture to industry inside the same area has consequences for family structures and relations. The average size of the family (4.1 in Bassano and 3.4 in Valdelsa), and the average number of working household members, continues to be large. Most of those working are employed in non-agricultural sectors. To this it must be added that about half the workers in the two districts said that they have close (non-cohabiting) siblings with whom they exchange different sorts of help. There were also found to be a good number of workers who declared that they have many friends with whom they exchange help and advice.

This is the overall context which must be borne in mind when we consider the substantial level of savings of the families; more than two-thirds of them had been able to save part of their income in the year preceding the poll. In the light of the data, it can therefore be said that the family and community institutional context – which was shaped by the previous agrarian structure – has not been radically uprooted by small-firm development. This context gives workers access to substantial resources which make possible the maintenance of a degree of independence from the conditions of the labour market. It also favours the ability of the individual – with the help of his family – to adapt to the need for the mobility and flexibility which are proper to small production units.

The large percentage of workers who stated that they have frequent and friendly relationships with non-cohabiting relatives, and the existence of networks of acquaintances where different social groups are involved suggest that family and community continue to have a relevant role in the shaping of individual behaviour. This factor, together with the close personal relationships within the firms and the high rates of social mobility, prevents the formation of deep class cleavages.

Autonomous working conditions

The process of production in small units leaves the individual worker a greater scope for self-management in comparison with the more rigid organisation which is typical of large firms. The data show a prevailing presence of fairly skilled tasks in both districts, but the traditional craft versions (on-the-job know-how and ability to perform different tasks) are more widespread than the modern ones (control of complex machinery). The former may not usually require a high level of technical skill, but may, nevertheless, involve some relative autonomy of the worker in the process of production (this is another factor which limits the proletarianisation of workers).

Some confirmation of the craft-type organisation may be derived from the judgements the workers made about various aspects of their work. Eighty per cent of Bassano workers and 75 per cent of the Valdelsa workers found their work interesting. Job security was evaluated as high by 70 per cent of all those interviewed and contractual conditions were considered good. The work was considered well or fairly well paid by 66 per cent of workers in Bassano and by 49 per cent in Valdelsa. On the negative side, 42 per cent of workers in Bassano found the work tiring and dangerous or harmful, while an even worse judgement (53 per cent) was given by those in Valdelsa.

Taken as a whole, these data give us a picture of a largely positive attitude towards the jobs carried out which, in the light of the most widespread tasks, seems to be related more to aspects of self-management than simply to matters of skills. It is likely that these judgements are affected by the informal relationships and the general 'climate' existing in small factories. In connection with this, one has to consider that 80 per cent of those interviewed in Valdelsa and 65 per cent in Bassano declared that 'relationships between people in our work place are usually co-operative: we quite often help one another'.

An enterprise culture

The majority of workers appear to appreciate the 'spirit of enterprise' and the role of the small entrepreneurs who are seen as active agents in the district model of development. A typical component of Social-Communist and Catholic cultures is, therefore, widespread in the areas under scrutiny. We found no evidence supporting an interpretation of this response as 'traditional deferential' (Lockwood, 1966), that is, as a consensus based on a shared system of values, whereby entrepreneurs are given an exclusive role of guidance in exchange for protection, following a typically paternalistic model. Most workers interviewed were found not to subscribe to this model. They did not agree with the statement: 'local entrepreneurs try to favour workers; they help them out of difficulties, and are also prepared to make sacrifices before resorting to dismissals'.

Consensus on entrepreneurs as organisers of production activities is not followed by an unconditional acceptance of the market as a regulating mechanism. Only 40 per cent of workers in Bassano and 30 per cent in Valdelsa were prepared to have incomes and employment levels dependent on the business cycle. Consistent with this was the common awareness of the negative side of working in the small firms.

All this suggests the existence of a sort of 'contractual' consensus to the district model of development; that is, an agreement based on a concrete evaluation of the advantages and disadvantages which the model is able to generate.[2] This is a generalised tendency. In neither contexts did a strong critical attitude towards production relations emerge. All the same, Tuscan workers seemed to be more reluctant to accept the market as a regulator of employment and income levels, and to pay greater attention to the negative side of their work relations. This difference does not seem to be explained by living and working conditions, which appear to be largely similar in the two districts. One explanatory factor is the continuing existence in the Veneto area of stronger ties with agriculture, together with a lower concentration of settlements in urban centres; but this alone cannot explain the observed differences in attitudes. These are much more likely to reflect the different effects of the Socio-Communist and Catholic cultures in the two areas. One can presume that the more critical attitude shown by Tuscan workers is connected with greater expectations of political regulation, while traditional 'background' resources continue to be relatively more relevant in the 'white' area.

Apart from such differences the analysed data have revealed that in any case the diffuse industrialisation has generated only limited proletarianisation. A considerable economic transformation has occurred without any violent social upheaval, and without causing marked social divisions likely to jeopardise the basis for a reproduction of political subcultures. This outcome has been fostered by processes of coordination and mediation between interests

which the subcultures themselves allowed for, and which we are
now going to examine.

Industrial relations

TRADE UNION ORGANISATION

While the role of the social and cultural context is largely recognised, the characteristics of industrial relations in areas with a
diffused economy are less well known. An image of 'weakness' of
trade union organisations usually prevails, but this is not
confirmed by the research data.

The rate of union membership among workers in the two areas
was ascertained as being 80 per cent in Valdelsa and 48 per cent in
Bassano. As might be expected, values rise with the size of the firm.
Almost all the Tuscan workers in firms with more than 50 employees are trade union members, while membership in firms of that
size is also very widespread in the Bassano area. In the size bracket
which is crucial for the economy of both districts – firms with 10 to
50 employees – the rate reaches 90 per cent in Valdelsa and 43 per
cent in Bassano. In smaller, artisan-like firms in the Bassano area
only a minority of workers (17 per cent) belongs to a union, while
40 per cent do so in the Valdelsa area. Of the unions, CGIL (the
Communist and Socialist union) is a near monopolist in the 'red'
area and CISL (of a Catholic bent) has the majority in the 'white'
area, but it is not as dominant.

Negotiations in 80 per cent of industrial firms in the sample in
Valdelsa, and 60 per cent in Bassano are controlled by the unions –
mostly via the factory council, but also with the participation of
union representatives in some firms. The scope of union negotiations can be assessed from information taken from the sample of
workers. Such negotiations involve about 70 per cent of the Tuscan
workers and rather more than 50 per cent of the Veneto ones. They
involve the industrial sector almost exclusively, that is all firms with
more than 10 employees (non-artisan firms), and are particularly
important in larger firms. In the 11 to 50 employees size bracket,
union negotiations involve 84 per cent of workers in Valdelsa, and
49 per cent in Bassano; in the 50 employees or over size bracket,
the figures are 97 per cent and 83 per cent, respectively.

NEGOTIATED ISSUES

In respect of the issues which are subject to negotiation, it can be seen that wages are of central relevance. This is even more apparent in Bassano. In the Tuscan area the average level of wages was estimated to be 19 per cent higher in the furniture sector and 15 per cent higher in machine tools and glass than the standard levels fixed by the national general contracts. In respect of the Veneto district, the average level of firm wages, for the same task levels, was 10 per cent above the national standard for furniture, and 6 per cent for clothing and shoes.

Another issue present in firm agreements is that of schedules and overtime. In our research it appeared in 84 per cent of cases in Valdelsa, and in 40 per cent in Bassano. The main difference between the two districts consisted of a greater number of clauses concerning overtime work, shifts, and compensating periods of rest in Valdelsa. However, this difference did not seem to affect the actual patterns of hours worked, nor the more general modes of labour force utilisation. Ninety-four per cent of respondents in Valdelsa, and 86 per cent in Bassano declared that they normally worked eight hours. On the other hand, a quarter of the respondants worked for nine or more hours 'during busy periods', stretching from one to three months. Twenty-five per cent of Tuscan workers and 36 per cent of Veneto workers also declared that they worked on Saturdays or during holidays, but many of these did so only occasionally. It can be added to this that 30 per cent of workers in both areas 'stayed at home for some time during the last few years, due to declining production.

All in all, the data does not reveal the existence of strong working time differences between the two districts. The most striking feature is, rather, that times and modes of labour force utilisation were objects of more active contractual negotiations in the Tuscan area; and that this was followed by more markedly beneficial results in terms of wages an job hierarchies.

FLEXIBILITY

Labour flexibility appears to be high in both areas, but it has not reached the levels which are often believed to occur. This flexibility seems to have been more a result of negotiations, with the Tuscans receiving better compensation. This interpretation receives indirect confirmation from indicators of labour mobility. About the same number of respondants (56 per cent in Valdelsa and 57 per cent in Bassano) had had one to three jobs in other firms before their present position, and 10 per cent more than three. Only a minority of those who changed jobs mentioned dismissal explicitly

as the reason for change. Rather they stressed reasons such as
voluntary choice and a search for better paid and safer occupa-
tions. The data revealed that labour force mobility has certainly
been an important factor in local economic development.
Differences between smaller, artisan-like firms and industrial ones
do not appear to be particularly marked. Flexibility seems to be a
distinguishing feature of the local system of production in its
entirety, although it is certainly better compensated in industrial
firms.

Work and politics

The small-firm economy can take many different forms. Research
work carried out in Italy on this topic has shown the importance of
a particular form which is based on the industrial district and
which is characterised by a specific institutional context. Labour
relations in these settings are 'shaped' by cultural, social and political factors which were forged in the long term. However, clarifying
the quality of work and unravelling its intricate relationship with
politics can help locate the Third Italy's experience in a comparative perspective.

The quality of work

The story of these districts – as well as that of other areas that have
been examined – suggests that they cannot usually be considered
as high-tech districts in which small units largely utilise the new
computer-based technologies such as numerically controlled
machines and other forms of sophisticated flexible equipment.
Rather we find small firms that are specialised in the production of
non-standard goods, but that usually rely on more traditional
multi-purpose technologies and craft-like skills. This does not
mean that the new electronic technologies are absent from the
districts or that they are not growing. So far, however, their diffusion remains limited, with important exceptions such as that of
machine-tool districts, especially in Emilia–Romagna (Perulli,
1989). In other industries – for example in textiles, clothing,
footwear – it has been more often a question of a blending of old
and new technologies. In any case, from an economic point of
view, the characteristics of technological equipment require careful

evaluation. In many cases, multi-purpose machines – even though they are not based on new technologies – can remain particularly suitable in the short run (Brusco, 1986). However, what mainly interests us here is the impact of the prevailing equipment on the quality of work.

It is usually recognised that an assessment of the quality of work clearly requires a multidimensional evaluation. It certainly involves psychophysiological aspects as well as other features such as work environment, level of skills, autonomy in the productive process, and chances of social mobility. But one should not neglect that work experience is also significantly shaped by the cultural, social and political environment external to the factory. From this perspective, other dimensions should be considered: the influence over living conditions – both cultural and material – of factors such as the family and local community, industrial relations and the activities of local government. Evaluation of the quality of work is therefore particularly complex and caution is required in any generalisation. However, a sketchy framework may be proposed in the following terms.

First, 'working hard' seems to be the rule in the two districts. However, it is related more to working time than to a rigid labour organisation. In addition, working hard becomes less important in the more advanced small firms, in which the available equipment limits the need for a 'quantitative' flexibility. The latter is more dependent on a flexible organisation of labour and higher levels of skill. In respect of safety and health, in general workers are not exposed to extreme risks. Both aspects, however, could entail serious problems and are objects of growing concern for the workers.

Workers' skills are obviously influenced by the above-mentioned features of the technological equipment. In this respect, one has to take into account that significant sectoral differences exist. But, on average, only a minority of workers possess high levels of technical skills, such as those involved in the ability to control complex machinery. In addition, there are very few managers and white-collar workers. At the same time, the small firms in three districts rely on a pool of unskilled labour which should not be overlooked. However, the standard pattern seems to involve a widespread presence of fairly skilled workers of the traditional kind (craft-like skills and ability to perform different tasks).

If one considers the autonomy of workers, the picture becomes even more different from that prevailing in mass production. As a matter of fact, the most distinctive feature of the quality of work in the districts is the higher degree of autonomy that the workers in small firms enjoy in comparison with their colleagues in the large mass-production firms. It is the limited subdivision of the productive process into rigid tasks, more than the level of technical skill, that mainly characterises the work experience there. In addition, one has to consider the higher rates of occupational and social mobility that the small-firm workers enjoy. Even though the real chances of mobility – especially in terms of a shift to an independent entrepreneurial position – seem to decrease over time, this aspect significantly affects the expectations and attitudes of workers.

Within the industrial district, market mechanisms and social institutions such as the family, the kinship network and the local community are closely interwoven. These social institutions provide cultural and material resources for the development of entrepreneurship and flexible productive structures. They motivate people to start new activities and help them to sustain the costs of setting up and operating small firms. At the same time, they also mitigate the effects on industrial workers of greater small firm discontinuity of employment and working time, and enable the costs of reproduction of labour to be lowered and incomes to be supplemented at the family level. Furthermore the persistence of community values which cut across social classes plays an integrative role that should not be underestimated in evaluating the 'success' of small-firm areas. Workers enjoy a low degree of proletarianisation, not only with reference to the organisation of labour and the chances for mobility, but also in relation to a working experience that does not entail a sharp uprooting from their original communities.

These social aspects of the small-firm economy are well known. The studies carried out in Valdelsa and Bassano also confirm that they are of great importance. Nevertheless, the insistence on the role of traditional institutions and identities runs the risk of being misleading, especially when it is applied to those areas where industrialisation is more consolidated and where there is a well-established political subculture. In these situations, the role played by a specific form of interest mediation, shaped through the influence of political subcultures on union representation and the activity of local government, must also be taken into consideration.

While the skills of small-firm workers are often overemphasised the level of wages is usually underestimated. The experience of the Third Italy suggests that small-firm development is not necessarily bound to low wages and to the evasion of labour regulations. Over time there has been an increase in real wages. In many districts, the average wages are currently above the standards which are fixed by the national agreements between unions and business associations. This is due to the influence on wages of agreements that are negotiated at a local level. Industrial relations therefore, play a role that should not be overlooked, one which is significantly affected by the institutional context in particular by the local political subcultures. In this respect, one has also to consider the activity of local government. The provision of services in the field of transport, housing, schools, daycare centres and health care have often anticipated or enriched national policies. Social services, therefore contribute significantly to improving the living conditions of the workers. In effect, these two districts benefit more than other areas from a kind of 'local social wage'. Together with the material effects of these policies the symbolic and cultural influence of local welfare is also to be considered: citizenship is enhanced by removing important areas of living standards, such as those relating to schooling, or to health, from the direct domain of the market. Again, one cannot understand these outcomes without considering the political context of the regions.

The role of politics can be analysed at two levels. First, it is important in shaping the peculiar equilibrium between the 'traditional' and 'modern' components that characterise these districts and affect labour relations and which help to explain the origins and particular locations of small-firm development in the Third Italy's regions. Second, politics strongly influence the operation of districts through industrial relations and the activities of local government.

Politics and the origins of the institutional context

The Italian literature clearly indicates that there is a relationship between small-firm growth and the social context in which it occurs. Among the factors which have attracted attention one finds: the agrarian class structure with a strong presence of non-waged work (sharecropping, peasant, and tenant farming); the persistence of extended families and local communities; and a tight network of small artisan and commercial centres. As a result of the combination of these factors a peculiar equilibrium between traditional and modern components has emerged over time. One could also say that the two regions have been able to avoid mass production with all its social, cultural and political effects.

However, one cannot understand the formation and the persistence of the social equilibrium of these regions – and therefore the origins and the location of industrial districts – without taking into account the political context. What has been the role of political subcultures in this process? The development of the Socialist and Catholic movements at the end of the nineteenth century was certainly influenced by the social structure which favoured the transformation of these movements into territorial political structures. Both of them cut across class boundaries and assumed wider community dimensions. Both of them shared a particular feature: they tried, although in different ways, to defend the local society[3] from the penetration of the market and of the national state; they tried to contain social disintegration and proletarianisation by experimenting with localised forms of organisation. As a matter of fact, the exclusion of the Socialists and Catholics from central political power led them to strengthen their positions at a local level, where conditions were more favourable.

In the 'red' areas, a tight network of unions, friendly societies and cooperatives developed in close collaboration with the Communists. The central regions were characterised by a lively 'Municipal Socialism'. In the 'white' areas of the north-east, unions were less present, but there was a network of rural savings and other banks, agricultural organisations, cooperatives, friendly societies, and charities, all of which were linked to the Church. It is not possible here to go into the details of the differences between the two subcultures – which, it should be said, are not to be underestimated – but at least three similar consequences of their influence on the model of economic growth should be considered.

First of all, both subcultures made an important contribution, through their organisations, to the formation and to the persistence of a social and cultural background based on a peculiar mix of traditional and modern components. They strengthened a localist kind of political economy and therefore preserved local communities and helped contain the erosion of productive relations based on non-waged work, both in the small towns (artisans) and in the country (sharecroppers and farmers). Second, and more specifically, they contributed to the high degree of legitimacy of entrepreneurship and to a work ethic which were very important later for small-firm growth. Third, they brought about an emancipation of the political system from civil society. Contrary to what happened in the south, where the Socialist and Catholic movements were very weak, politics became more autonomous from individual or family interests and more bound to the defence of collective interests, even though with a strong localist connotation. Again, this factor was a crucial legacy which helped the political economy of the small-firm areas.

Industrial relations and local government activities

In Italy the debate on industrial relations has centred mainly on the experience of large firms and on the central political system. This brought about a long-lasting distortion. Productive structures different from the large industrial firms were usually considered as if they were not covered by industrial relations. However, research conducted in small-firm areas in the early 1980s provided evidence which questioned an interpretation of labour relations conceived in terms of 'dualism' (Goldthorpe, 1984). In order to understand this neglect of industrial relations in small and medium-sized firms, one has probably to consider that in the Italian debate industrial relations are often synonymous with conflictual industrial relations. Since the prevailing model of industrial relations in small firms is not conflictual, it is usually thought that in these settings there are no industrial relations at all.

What is the prevailing model of industrial relations in the small-firm areas, especially in the central and north-eastern regions? First, the rate of unionisation grew significantly in the 1970s, and it was always higher than in the large firms of the north-west (the average rate of unionisation for the two major unions – CGIL and CISL – reached almost 50 per cent of industrial workers in the central regions and almost 40 per cent in the north-eastern regions, while in the regions of mass production, the rate of unionisation was less than 30 per cent). In the 1980s there was a decline, though it was not as strong as that in the large-firm areas. The research conducted in industrial districts has shown that unionisation was fostered by the particular features of the local political systems. Political traditions provided identity and organisational resources which facilitated unionisation, in spite of the very fragmented productive structure. The stronger were the political subcultures, the more unionisation increased.

Of course, one could remark – as many observers did in Italy – that this kind of unionisation is bound to have a subcultural character, with limited effects on industrial relations. But there is evidence to show that although this was true in the initial stages of small-firm growth – in the 1960s and early 1970s – in the following period unions exploited their organisational resources and acquired increasing autonomy from political parties. Again, there are differences between 'red' and 'white' areas (for example, unionisation is higher in the 'red' areas), but in both cases a specific model of industrial relations, different from that prevailing in large firms, was triggered off. This is a cooperative and localist model. Unions have not placed constraints on the flexible use of labour – both within and among the local firms – in exchange for increases in local wages, the maintenance of full employment at the local level, and the provision of welfare benefits by local governments. The territorial level of unions is usually more important than the firm level for bargaining local agreements, although in some districts agreements at firm level are also significant (usually in non-artisan firms with more than 20 employees). In such cases, for example, aspects related to flexibility and work organisation can be directly negotiated by members of the works councils and the employers (Perulli, 1989). In general, the model is based on what we could call a 'compensated flexibility'. Unions contribute indirectly to the social acceptance of high labour flexibility by raising its wage value, but without negotiating its actual implementation, which is more frequently left to direct agreements between workers and their employers.

Two main factors fostered the institutionalisation of this model. The first is related to the social and cultural features of the working class which we have already considered; in particular, the low proletarianisation of this social group which derives from the prevailing organisation of work in the small firms, from deep-rooted family and community ties, and from the high opportunities for social mobility. These factors have not favoured the kind of militant unionism and conflictual relations that prevail in large firms and industrial cities.

The second aspect is related to the activities of the local governments. In the small-firm areas local governments have usually been able to provide a certain quantity of collective goods which have reduced costs for both employers and workers, and which have thereby encouraged local compromise. These goods include social services for workers (transport, public housing, schools, daycare centres) and, for local firms, the provision of industrial estates, infrastructures, professional training, and support to consortia for marketing or export facilities. Communities also have become increasingly involved in attempts to find solutions to crises in those firms which are particularly important to the economy of the area. This has often involved putting pressure on regional and national governments to grant redundancy payments to the workers and even interceding with local banks on questions of credit. It has also involved mediating between local unions and entrepreneurs. Communities, however, have limited powers in the economic field. Their social policies have had a much greater impact. Again, there are differences which cannot be considered in detail here. Suffice it to say that the 'red' administrations have tended, on the whole, to be more interventionist, while the 'white' ones have been less interventionist in land use and urban policies and have delegated most social services to the network of Catholic associations; the former have tried to increase the regulative role of politics, while the latter have been more oriented towards sustaining traditional institutions.

Why have local governments in these regions been able to play the role described above? Two aspects should be considered. First, contrary to what has happened in other areas, political subcultures have provided generalised support which has freed local leaders from the concerns of particular and fragmented demands. Success has been more dependent on the ability to provide collective goods for the local community. Clientism has been contained. Second, the diffuse character of industrialisation, especially in its initial states has limited the problems that local governments have had to face. That the traditional family and the community background have not changed dramatically, that there has been no great inflow of immigrants, and that employment and consumption have been sustained, has not only facilitated the task of local administrators, but has also allowed traditional institutions to be used as regulative resources.

On the whole, the influence of the political context on industrial relations and local government activity has helped to establish a social compromise based, on the one hand, on the high flexibility of the economy and, on the other, on the control of costs and the redistribution of the benefits accruing from economic growth. Politics have been able to play this role by combining traditional and modern regulative resources. However, the institutional context that has emerged in this process is not to be considered as a set of external conditions facilitating the working of the market. Our areas cannot be described in terms of a *laissez-faire* society. Borrowing from Dore [1986], we could rather define the role of social and political institutions in terms of 'flexible rigidities'. Economic relationships have been shaped by social and political mechanisms which limit the role and scope of the market. But in this way they have fostered flexibility and the ability of the local economy to innovate.

A final remark. It is appropriate to emphasise the local dimension of the small-firm political economy in the Third Italy. The economic, social and political resources that have affected the operation of industrial districts have been mostly endogenous. This aspect is important because it could offer a key to the problems of modernisation that are likely to affect the, small-firm areas in the future. Of course, this point deserves a more specific treatment, but I wish to conclude by mentioning that new problems are now menacing the localist kind of political economy that we have described. There is, therefore, a need for new research in this field.

An aspect which should probably attract attention is the emergence of new types of external economies and diseconomies which cannot be easily dealt with at a local level. For example, on the one hand, problems of innovation are emerging that require resources that are not always available at the local level: technological research and information, marketing and export services, more sophisticated financial services, managerial and labour training. On the other hand, new external diseconomies have clearly appeared: pollution, waste disposal, traffic congestion and transport, energy supply. Again, it is difficult to tackle these problems only at a local level and with endogenous resources. In other words, it seems that the development of industrial districts is facing a problem of scale. Constraints of scale make the local economy more dependent on a wider mode of regulation of a regional kind. This is not to say, however, that industrial districts are bound to become less important as institutional forms of economic organisation. What is hypothesised is that they could probably consolidate their role if the original isolation was broken and new, more complex, forms of interaction and co-operation were built. However, it is worth considering that, in this regard, the strong local aspect of the industrial districts political economy could change status: from a fast source of strength to a menacing future constraint.

Notes

1. For a comprehensive picture of the research programme, see Bagnasco and Trigilia (1984, 1985, 1993).
2. The notion of a negotiated adaptation of the working class to capitalistic social relationships has been employed by Parkin (1971).
3. I use this concept in the sense proposed by Polanyi (1944).

3

LOCAL PRODUCTIVE SYSTEMS AND NEW INDUSTRIAL POLICY IN ITALY

SEBASTIANO BRUSCO

The need to generalise results obtained from a study of industrial districts

In recent years, especially in Italy, analytical work carried out in industrial districts has refocused the attention of economists and, more generally, of social scientists on the role that factors usually defined as 'extra economic' have on the productivity of the economic system and on the organisation of work within the industrial business. (It would be very interesting to go over past discussions on these topics, but to embark on the subject would entail too much time and this is not the right forum to do so.)

During this discussion it has been emphasised how important consensus and social cohesion are to engender that mixture of competition and cooperation among businesses that is deemed increasingly necessary for the establishment of an environment which encourages high productivity and frequent innovation. As shown by Fiorani, Franchi and Rieser (1993) there is now agreement on the fact that these conditions are perfectly compatible with a strong dialectic among the business partners and that they can even encourage the emergence among businesses of a mixture of conflict and active cooperation – somewhat in parallel to that mentioned above – which is necessary for production at a level of total quality.

However, this is not the whole question. More widely, reference by Becattini (1990) to a 'Marshallian' atmosphere, studies by Bagnasco and Trigilia on the relationship between economic and political systems, the attention called to the role played by local authorities, analysis of social mobility and its consequences for the productivity of the system as a whole and of the individual business, research on the nature and implications of 'trust' – being only some of the topics studied by researchers working on industrial districts – have brought forward a crop of results that precisely reassert the central role in economic activity played by factors not normally taken into consideration by economic analysis.

As a result of this line of research and in view of the fact that other intellectual paths have led to the same conclusion, many scholars and politicians today believe that economic success is not linked only to a few fundamental economic parameters (which range from the exchange rate to salary, from interest rate to consumers' tendencies and to investment rate) but depends, on the contrary, and crucially, on other variables.

Towards a definition of local productive systems

Perhaps the time has come, at this stage, to ask oneself to what extent experience gained in the study of industrial districts may be extended to all local productive systems. In other words, it must be ascertained whether each zone delimited in some way – with its delimitation remaining a problem to be looked at carefully – could usefully be considered as a unit for analysis and for planning any intervention, even if the district might not have the characteristics of an industrial district. If this exercise had a theoretical basis, Becattini's theorem ('Besides the business and the sector, a third element of analysis, with a strong territorial feature, has a theoretical basis: the industrial zone') could be reformulated in a more general way by placing alongside business and sector, in the list of components of a national economy, local productive systems, of which the districts would represent a defined prototype.

From this viewpoint, a local productive system can be defined as a system composed of three principal elements: the active businesses, the territory in which they are located and the people living in that territory, with their values and their history, which is also the history of the businesses, the signs of which are imprinted on the land. Distinctive characteristics for defining the system boundaries – which do not, of course, necessarily, coincide with administrative boundaries – are the strong connections among businesses and the relative homogeneity of the social system.

It is evident that the definition is very wide. Silicon Valley can be considered a local productive system with its scores of businesses, large and small, recently or less recently established, which strongly interact among themselves and with the universities; or the area around Treviso where the Benetton industrial group networks with a large number of small and medium-size businesses; or areas like Barcelona or Bologna, where different industrial sectors share the same set of values and the same style of work and life; or the city of Turin which is a classic company town, or of course, Carpi or Prato – which have all the features of an industrial district. Therefore, an extraordinary variety of productive linkages exist which, presumably, as Scott and Storper have tried to do, can be reduced to a relatively simple classification.

Local productive systems can be very different from one another, not only concerning the productive apparatus, but also with reference to the social structures of which they are constituted. The events by which each community has built its own set of values are very diverse. There are innumerable axes around which communities, even of recent formation, find cohesion and solidarity: ranging from parochialism to trade associations, from Little Italy to China town, to the homogeneity of political creed in the Emilian and Veneto regions. It should also be reiterated that the idea of a compact social structure does not imply an absence of clashes of interest or conflict and that a local productive system, as defined, can be characterised, as in certain southern Italian regions, by a social situation which is highly disintegrated, or even by the presence of a booming illegal economy.

In essence, therefore, the definition of local productive system proposed is very general and the elements that characterize such a system are only the strong relationships among businesses and the homogeneity of the social structure.

Local productive systems are different and stable

The analytical relevance of the definition proposed above depends crucially on two conditions: that local productive systems are different from one another – with respect to both the productive apparatus and the social structure – and that they are relatively stable in time. If this were not the case, it would not be possible to differentiate them and not worthwhile studying them in depth.

Many elements, however, lead one to think that such conditions are valid. The characteristics of the productive apparatus and social structure, in effect, are both strictly linked to what Braudel called 'the level of material life'. The examples one can refer to are numerous. One needs only to think of the way in which family structures (patriarchal or one-parent families) can influence the system of pensions and hence the cost of work, or how much the expansion of social services and the rate of women's activity and employment affect wages. Certainly family structures and the division of work among the sexes have strong effects on the founding of businesses, on social mobility and, therefore, indirectly on the state of industrial relations, on the popularity of auto-consumption and 'do-it-yourself' and on the structure of tertiary services: ranging from fast foods to launderettes to plumbers. To simplify drastically the rich articulation of Braudel's proposal, one can perhaps say that long-lasting elements decisively affect the processes of reproduction of the workforce, saving and capital accumulation even in an advanced capitalist system.

In a similar way, long-lasting structures govern the quality of consolidated knowledge in the social structure, which derives from experience gained in the workplace from professional training and research: this knowledge in turn is a crucial influence on the capacity for competition and innovation. Long-term structures also determine the quality of trust and market trends which affect so markedly the costs of all transactions and the levels of cooperation among businesses.

The conditions of material life, in brief, affect strongly the modes of reproduction of the workforce, levels, rhythms and channels of accumulation of knowledge and the characteristics of the markets. It is this strong relationship which justifies both the difference between various local productive systems and their stability through time, and which safeguards those conditions, thus allowing local productive systems to be accredited as a unit of analysis and in the planning of interventions.

Distinctive characteristics of districts as a basis for an evaluation of local productive systems

As seen above, from theoretical results obtained from a study of the districts, the idea of a new unit of analysis can be derived: that, precisely, of local productive systems. However, one can go further. The analysis of districts, in effect, can provide some useful tools to investigate the proposed new units and to evaluate them for their efficiency and competitive capability. Many of the results obtained during the analysis of the districts can be summarised in a very simple scheme, according to which the 'quality' of the district depends on certain crucial factors. These factors can be summarised by three principal points:

1. The relationships among businesses are characterised by a close interweaving of competition and cooperation.
2. The relationships between entrepreneurs and their employees – both at the micro-level within the business and at the macro-level in industrial relations – present at any one time elements of conflict and elements of participation.
3. The productive and, more generally, the social structure are rich in knowledge closely connected with productive activity, technology, marketing and often financial administration and management.

The following paragraphs are given to the discussion of these points and to the manner in which these characteristics can be developed, upheld and strengthened, with reference to specific local productive systems.

Competition and cooperation

Besides the factors mentioned above, there is a further advantage for businesses in the districts: the very high number of operators, each one with his own market strategy and specialisation which ensures the client easy availability – within a restricted area – of products from a variety of sources and market levels. In the textile sector, for example, it would easily be possible to find wool and cotton or synthetic products for man, woman and child, of medium high or very high quality, of classical style or the latest fashion. This results in effect, in a sort of 'trade fair' with the difference that this fair, contrary to traditional ones, is open during the whole buying season, or during the whole year, and it exercises on buyers a considerable promotional impact.

In brief, therefore, the businesses in the districts enjoy an advantage as compared to their sister businesses operating elsewhere. We can probably sustain the view that their profits are, on average, higher and that they can overcome more easily periods of crisis: this is indeed the reason why small businesses in Carpi or Prato are often in a position to compete with larger businesses operating elsewhere.

Despite all this, there are no signs of collusion in the districts. End suppliers (i.e. those that have responsibility for the production and sale of the finished product) compete in a lively way among themselves in the product market regarding price, delivery time, after-sales service, intrinsic quality and quality of design. Innovations are frequent and there are no qualms in adopting a good design or technical improvement devised by another company, should this prove technically feasible. The physical proximity of businesses and the large number of personal contacts among entrepreneurs and employees gives a transparency to prices for all buyers, thus strengthening the image of a 'fair' mentioned before. Good and bad features of each company are known by most, if not by all the others, and any agreements whether secret or open are made impossible by the large number of agents. The extraordinary ease of access, the high rate of founding and demise of companies, the urge for personal success, all these factors ensure that any excess profits are temporary and rapidly eliminated.

The natural progression is that if one wishes to succeed in a market, one must use the same weapons as the competition, such as price, design, etc. thereby passing on to consumers the advantages of belonging to a zone. This very lively competition is not in contradiction with the many forms of cooperation. A classification of the various forms of cooperation is virtually impossible. An attempt can only be made to study the most frequent cases, grouping them according to the economic function which faces them.

To start with, many entrepreneurs are related simply by friendly behaviour, as in the case when very small businesses lend each other tools, or raw materials not easily available on the market. It often happens that in order to meet a particularly important order or a delivery within a short time, a business requests the cooperation of a competitor. This can be effected either through a formal arrangement (when both businesses agree to accept the order) or through an informal agreement (when only one business accepts responsibility towards the client guaranteeing quality and delivery time for the whole order). The logic behind such agreements is obvious and lies in the fact that cooperation is only temporary, the roles are interchangeable and each business is able to meet the occasional order in excess of its productive capacity, or the productive capacity available after existing orders are met.

Another frequent form of cooperation among businesses is often responsible in great measure for the innovative capability of the zone. We refer to the relationship between the client and the components manufacturer. Very often a spare part or a component is not ordered on the basis of a precise design with detailed specifications. Instead, the client explains to a subcontractor the function of the part and is ready to discuss the possible use of a standard part, which is already available on the market and therefore cheaper, to perform the task, or to discuss the feasibility of producing the part but with modifications compared to the original requirements that make it easier to produce. The relationship which forms the basis of the order has a strong consultancy element and this is particularly so when the component manufacturer is a producer of moulds. In fact, moulds are rarely ordered on the basis of precise drawings. More often the client requests the reproduction of a certain part which he brings along as a prototype, but is prepared to modify it if this allows a reduction in costs without loss of efficiency. In some instances, expanding on the given example, cooperation between client and supplier can result in substantial modifications to the finished product, thus promoting technical innovations which are nearly always of an incremental type, but are still of considerable value in the market.

The reasons why a manufacturer of moulds or any other subcontractor is so generous with his time and makes himself so readily available to study a problem which, after all, is not his, are various and not necessarily mutually exclusive. It may be that the goodwill demonstrated on one occasion may be good publicity for future orders. Furthermore, information at our disposal shows that consultancy time is included as part of the general costs so that in the end, the clients divide the cost among themselves by whatever formula is used. This does not exclude, however, the desirability of more consultancy (with the direct costs increased by higher general expenses) rather than less consultancy and a lower increase on the direct costs. It is also true that the direct costs themselves may also be reduced, precisely because of the discussions and dialogue.

Other forms of cooperation, differing from the ones described above, involve many businesses and these require an agent to coordinate them. The most common cases are purchase consortia, where many businesses join up to obtain their input at a lower price; credit consortia, where several businesses band together to guarantee each other's bank loans or to negotiate a lower bank interest rate; agencies, often represented in Italy by trade associations, which keep the books and payrolls for member businesses and compile their income return forms at a very low cost. In addition, trade associations often coordinate groups of members to reduce the costs of participation in trade fairs, or to promote regional products, or to acquire the necessary sites to develop their businesses or to build – together and therefore more economically – the structures that will house their factories. The classic role played by trade associations, of trade union representation and trade representation with government authorities, can also be considered a mode of cooperation.

The factors which lead to the formation of such consortia are easily understood and recognisable. In fact some functions such as bookkeeping or the purchase of input could not be undertaken efficiently within the individual business in the case of a very small company. The consortia described – or equivalent organisations – simply represent the only way in which small businesses once again stand a chance of operating efficiently at a minimum viable level in whatever sector. The objective is, therefore, to be able to take advantage of all possible economies of scale, be these concrete, as in the case of bookkeeping or the construction of physical structures, or pecuniary, as in the case of purchase and credit consortia.

Furthermore, small businesses can join up or be encouraged to work together to achieve other aims which are more immediately connected with the urgent need to utilise new technologies and to reach new markets. The problems originating from sharing these services – which could be defined as 'superior' or advanced – will be examined in detail in the second part of this chapter.

Finally, one must not forget those types of cooperation among businesses which have been formalised: recent research on small ironworks businesses in Modena shows that out of 220 businesses interviewed 30 per cent have involvement in other businesses operating within the same sector. It is not unlikely that the exchange of stocks/shares between companies that hold shares in each other businesses entails not only cooperation but also coordination.

Relationships between entrepreneurs and employees within a business and industrial reactions: conflict and active cooperation

The second element which distinguishes those districts with a successful history has to do with relationships internal to the business and more generally relationships between entrepreneurs and employees. In the past it has been said that trade unions in developed districts are 'strong and reasonable': sufficiently strong, in fact, not to allow less than decent working conditions and salaries lower than those of the various national contracts, but reasonable enough never to induce, not even during the most heated trade union struggles, Luddite practices, and never to impose working conditions or pay levels much higher than the national average. A good example of this climate of relationships can be found in the working contracts of the artisanal sector. The first contract drawn up in Italy between artisanal unions and trade unions was in 1962 and was signed in Modena. The first regional contract was also signed in Emilia in 1970 and only a few years later this type of agreement spread to Lombardy and Veneto. However, these contracts, although strongly innovative, certainly did not have a revolutionary tone; they simply aimed at extending to the artisanal sector the working conditions agreed upon for large businesses, between the Confederation of Indusry and the Confederations of Trade Unions.

In the history of the industrial districts in Emilia there are many examples of this mixture of a high level of unionisation and a commitment to efficiency. At the beginning of the 1950s, for example, cooperatives of labourers in Modena, after a long period of hard struggle against landowners, adopted on many occasions clearly maximalist positions. The cooperatives even sustained that 'land is conquered, not bought' and they refused to use the provisions laid down by law for the creation of peasant ownerships, which conceded a 30-year mortgage at 1 per cent interest. However, at the same time, cooperatives moved towards a restructuring of dairy and consumer cooperatives, closing small dairy businesses and small village outlets which were a focal point of assembly, a place of gathering and discussion and a source of community pride. In order to attain higher levels of efficiency, these cooperatives were closed and absorbed by larger cooperatives with more productive machinery enabling them to compete with other businesses operating in the market.

The personal histories of artisanal entrepreneurs also encourage this kind of behaviour. The events that took place in the period following World War II, at Fiat in Modena and Officine Reggiane in Reggio are well known. The more unionised workers who were dismissed set up artisanal businesses of their own, often continuing to work for their old employers but as sub-contractors rather than employees. Even today, a high proportion of artisanal business is created by workers in their thirties who have learnt their trade as employees in other artisanal businesses, or in larger businesses. Workers who follow this career pattern generally possess high qualifications and, as often happens, are among the most active in trade unions; Once they become employers, they are naturally and obviously receptive to their employees' involvement with the unions and are prepared to discuss their work conditions. This is, in brief, an attempt to show that a typical entrepreneur in the districts is highly committed to efficiency and profit, but considers it only natural that his employees are members of trade unions and expect him to respect their contractual rights and set good working conditions. To oppose this would negate one's own history and values. The irremovable problem of the sharing out of the income produced by the business is of a different order from the problem of salary and working environment, which can be taken as a fixed factor set by external arbitration, such as the national contract.

According to a recent study by Maura Franchi (1990) from which the following quotations are taken; it can be affirmed that the fundamental points of reference become the organisation of work and patterns of internal mobility. The organisation of work is characterised by a low degree of sharing out of work. 'Each one is in charge of a principal task, but can occasionally be assigned to other tasks', often using less up-to-date machinery which is kept in use and maintained in operational order precisely because it gives flexibility to the industry. Workers are, therefore, not tied to a single machine, even if their polyvalency is 'differentiated, both horizontally, since there are obvious limits with different types of machinery and phases of the production cycle, and also vertically, because of a professional hierarchy'.

Internal mobility – with the exception of a small number of workers who can be defined, even though there is no legal basis for it, as occasional, temporary or migratory, – provides for three principal phases: 'on-the-job training, responsibility and co-optation'. The first phase is of vocational and apprenticeship training, more substantial and varied than in a large business. In fact, as shown by Brusco and Solinas (1993), the percentage of employees who become employers is higher in small businesses than in medium or large ones. After the training period, however informal it is, some workers take over key roles within the business. Among these some will end up by being co-opted by their employer as partners or assisted in starting a business of their own. What makes this important is the widespread presence of this phenomenon and the high number of workers involved. Fiorani, Franch and Rieser in their research already mentioned (1993) showed that out of 230 small ironwork industries in the Modena region between 1985 and 1992 a third acquired new partners, more than 40 per cent of whom came from within the businesses. In the same study it is demonstrated that 33 per cent of all entrepreneurs interviewed stated that they encouraged the creation of new businesses by guaranteeing orders, lending equipment, or giving financial help.

This whole process, which is often translated into terms of wages and position, rather than of a formalised framework 'is not regulated by rules contracted by trade unions, but largely depends on choices made directly by the entrepreneur.' To summarise, in this type of business, the management of the workforce is exercised above all through the control of the task assigned and career structure, and the employer makes his decisions on the basis of two principal criteria: reliability, which is fundamentally defined as the will to take over within limits the values and future outlook of the business, and professionalism. The employer has a greater legitimate right to value these elements because of the fact that he continues to do manual work, and in any case, he knows his craft well. These criteria are all the more justified since not only the efficiency, but also the innovative capacity of the business is based on them. The discretion enjoyed by the entrepreneur, though legitimate and justified, can in reality engender suspicion that in the businesses in question the relationships between employer and employees might be interpreted, not as so far sustained, in terms of cooperation and conflict, but rather and more usefully in terms of paternalism. The strong elements of informality that empirical research always shows could strengthen this hypothesis. On the other hand, within this regimen of industrial relationships, two of the key elements of paternalism are completely absent. There is in this context no occasion for transfer of resources other than salary, which is one of the key characteristics of paternalism. In other words, employers do not control their employees through the offer of housing, schools or summer camps for young children, scholarships for older children, medical assistance, etc. Furthermore, the most authentic sign of paternalism, hegemony, is lacking hegemony, intended exactly in the Gramscian sense of entrepreneur *vis-à-vis* deferential employee. It may be possible to sustain that the practice of formalised conflicts (for instance through participation in a strike to obtain a collective contract) when undertaken as a natural course of action without generating resentment and deep tensions is contradictory and incompatible with the phenomena of paternalism.

Knowledge consolidated in the social structure

The third element mentioned is represented by knowledge spread throughout the social structure of the district, which is embedded in the historical memory of men and women belonging to the district. This is certainly the most evident of the three factors for success in determining good results: the one most immediately perceived by researchers and operatives in the field of economics. Not only is the competence of the workers particularly high, but there is also in these districts planning ability, experience of import and export procedures, experience of different channels of sale, at least some awareness of problems connected with financial management and sometimes very precise knowledge of the state and characteristics of particular markets. In essence, it can be defined as a culture of planning, producing and selling. The point of this is that these abilities are present not only in the most advanced form in a few privileged individuals, but widely spread among hundreds or thousands of people who participate in the productive activity, by their engagement in the sector which characterises the district, or in some other activity within the productive apparatus. It is, in fact, the very rich interweaving of the relationships established among all these agents, more than the special contribution of individuals, that gives the district its competitiveness, innovative capacity, and, above all, that quick perception of opportunities for profit, the lack of which, according to Hirschman, plays a crucial role in explaining underdevelopment.

This ability to master techniques, in the wider sense of planning, innovation and selling, and not only of production, requires an important clarification. It is important, in other words, to remember that reference is not made to the ability to control and manage which, in traditional studies of economics, is represented and summarised by a production function. Here, on the contrary, reference is made to the technological path, to a whole system of knowledge that, though given and stable in its principles and fundamental methods, is still liable to further elaboration and is continually evolving. The 'know-how' in question has no relation to the productive process, but to a method of intricate paths and inter-relationships oriented to opening up new itineraries, or constructing new pathways. The width and depth of knowledge and the large number of people involved are, therefore, basic characteristics of this knowledge, which explains why this culture is so fertile and fruitful and so difficult to acquire. These are, for example, the reasons why the conversion from a mechanical to an electronic culture which has occurred in many districts has still not been fully accomplished.

New industrial policy and local productive systems

What are the implications of the discussion conducted so far on industrial policy? What initiatives should public authorities take to encourage growth in local productive systems? In previous paragraphs, it has been said that development depends crucially on a deep rooting within the communities concerned of those elements of knowledge, those values and judgement criteria that, as has been seen, represent factors which have contributed most to the success of some districts. Taking into account such beliefs, and comparing them to more traditional positions, industrial policies can be grouped into two large categories.

First, there are policies intended for individual businesses, which aim at increasing artificially the rate of profit from an investment or any other business initiative. The main instruments used in such cases are financial subsidies without security to a capital account or subsidies of various types aimed at reducing the cost of money borrowed from a bank. Such measures can yield very good results but only if a series of conditions are met. In particular, it is essential that the only or at least the main handicap for the businesses involved in this intervention, compared to their competitors, is that their rate of expected profit is too low to be worthwhile if the necessary initiatives are carried out at market prices. There are many reasons for this situation: the small size of the business, its location in the area or some other cause. The incentives given by the public have, as mentioned, the role of artificially increasing the rate of profit.

A policy built essentially on incentives presumes, therefore, that a solution to the problems referred to in previous paragraphs has been found, or at least that the problems have been reasonably identified and are on their way to being solved: the problem of opportunism in business relationships and the resulting difficulty of collaboration; the problem of relationships between employers and employees with the obstacles that these create for a fruitful participation in the work process; and the problem of easy access to knowledge. The assumption is that businesses could always count on finding within themselves, or externally, all the capabilities and competencies necessary to elaborate and put into practice appropriate strategies for the market in which they operate.

Furthermore, it is indeed upon these axes that the new industrial policy pivots. It does not necessarily substitute previous policy, but aims at acting, first of all, on the fundamental characteristics of the productive apparatus, in the knowledge that every local productive system is different from its neighbour, especially in view of their different municipal histories, and is affected by that sense of inertia typical of long-lasting situations which contributes to make it unreceptive to radical changes. Among other considerations, this is why it is not possible to resort to a manual of initiatives suitable for all occasions, and fitting all requirements, and reference can only be made to the objectives to be achieved and general principles that must guide the planning of any intervention. It might be useful, however, to refer here to some of the experience gained, evaluating it and looking for its theoretical bases.

In this study, however, an even more limited exercise is proposed. Not only will the discussion be conducted, as mentioned, nearly always through examples and references, but the problem of initiatives capable of stimulating the growth of a system of industrial relationships, in which conflict and active cooperation positively interact, will be left untouched. The subject is too vast and too full of implications to be attempted, even in synthesis, in this forum.

The following two concluding sections are devoted to initiatives that have as their objective the diffusion of cooperation and the increase of skills.

Towards the growth of cooperation

The initiatives essayed to encourage cooperation are extremely varied in nature. The decisive point is the reduction of opportunism. On the positive side one can speak of a growth in trust.

One can, perhaps, summarise all these initiatives under two principal headings although at times there is considerable overlap.

A first means of pursuing this objective is to improve the level of information. In economic jargon one speaks of diminishing the asymmetry of information. The establishment of agencies to spread reliable information on technology and markets; the creation of laboratories where it is easy to control the quality of input and output; the founding of specialised technical publications; organising collective visits to trade shows for the sector or guided tours of businesses in areas of success; approval of rules to be followed to obtain the establishment of marks of quality, which may be compulsory or optional and managed publicly or privately; the compilation and circulation of yearbooks detailing the principal features of businesses, possibly accompanied by reliable references; the institution of prizes of various types: for loyalty, length of service, high professional standards, punctuality in service, fairness of price: These are only some possible initiatives. The most effective and appropriate choice among those mentioned – or whatever others – can only be determined by analysing the specific business situation in which one operates. It is worth mentioning, partly in jest, that according to some sources the publication of the *Good Food Guide* has had important consequences on the standard of English restaurants. It is also useful to mention that many of the above initiatives, precisely because they lower the level of opportunism practicable without running risks, involve vast interests and encourage very bitter disputes: One need only think, for instance, of the many categories of producers who even today have successfully opposed common-sense rules dictating that the label on a product should state the composition, origin and production technique.

A second group of initiatives, on the other hand, as shown by Sabel (1992) in his analysis of the 'Studied Trust' aims at creating a group identity. Even in this case, circulation of information is greatly increased. However, here the principal objective is to stimulate the setting up of rules that value collaboration and penalise through social sanctions, which are no less effective for being informal, breaches of the code of correct behaviour. The cementing bond that links members of the group can be of different types. Political choice can be a factor, as has happened in Emilia among the supporters of the old Communist Party, or politico-religious as with the Christian Democrats in Veneto. It can be useful to encourage the expansion of business associations or even of trade corporations with characteristics reminiscent of the old guilds. In some cases, unity is attained as a result of racial situations or situations connected with national or local tradition. It does not follow, of course, that any type of aggregation is to be favoured; it often happens that the motive for aggregation becomes an occasion for narrow-mindness and collusion, hampering the more general development of the community of which the group forms a part.

In analysing and operating such interventions one point must be kept clearly in mind: the cooperation in question is never principally made up of goodwill, voluntarism or philanthropy. Of course, it can happen that this trust can also find its apostles, just as the Emilian cooperatives at Agnini and Prampolini found at the end of the last century. But now, as then, cooperation coexists with competition, with the opening of international markets, with the absence of collusion and with efficiency. Even though one cannot do without goodwill, collaboration means above all making a choice for a medium or long-term period, contrasted with the temptation of the 'grab your money and run' philosophy which governs the logic of quick profit.

Towards growth of competence

The second axis of intervention in the new industrial policy deals with the development of those businesses or productive structures that most urgently need to access the knowledge and competences which, in the pattern of incentives, were presumed to be readily available. More concretely, traditional industrial policy assumes that the business knows exactly what it should be producing and for which market and with which type of machinery. In the new perspective, the business must be helped to acquire the necessary instruments to make correct strategic decisions, or, more generally, to endow the productive network with the competence necessary to grasp the opportunities for profit offered by the more demanding markets. This second type of initiative – to explain further what might already be clear – has the principal objective of modifying the underlying structures of the productive and social network – to influence, that is, long-term structures already mentioned in previous paragraphs.

There are several ways to pursue this objective. In situations of relative under-development, such as that which exists in several areas of Southern Italy and in many depressed areas of Spain and

Greece, the key instrument is probably represented by the transfer to these areas of large industries capable of encouraging the growth of a web of sub-suppliers and willing to do so. Models in this direction have recently been proposed by Butera, Dioguarda and, abroad, though with different implications, by Lucas. Graziani, for instance, summarising Lucas' thought writes: 'the fact itself of being born and living in a certain society, makes one acquire a certain culture, accustoms the mind to the technologies in use, and predisposes the person to work according to the requirements which are in keeping with the modes prevailing in that society'. (Naturally, in order to induce large national industries to open large factories in the depressed areas of the country, a process of negotiation will be necessary and this might include financial incentives; but this is obviously a different case from that of the incentives granted to local businesses mentioned in previous paragraphs.)

Even in more developed areas, where the productive network is more vital and more responsive to stimulation, the arrival of a big business with strong innovative capabilities can have very considerable and positive effects. In this case other interventions can also be effective, interventions that while still operating along the line of modifying the existing conditions towards a line of modification of the underlying conditions of the productive and social networks aim to make readily available to businesses the real services needed to overcome bottlenecks, to adopt new technology, to acquire the knowledge necessary to operate with awareness and efficiency in one's own market. The underlying idea is that small and medium-sized businesses need, above all, to have readily available information relating to new technology, new standards, internal and external market movements and market trends. They also need assistance to interpret new laws, to create new organisational structures, to standardise their products, to adapt to their particular conditions the measures necessary for total quality; and they need to locate urgently an organisational forum to protect their interests in Rome or Brussels. These requirements can be met, either by departmental agencies, built on the model of the service centres of Ervet, or by sole-purpose agencies, like the certification centres, or sector monitoring centres. Public intervention in this case is not justified by claiming improved managerial capability or by deciding on a whim to experiment with new models of industrial relations, or control requirements, but only in the lack of capability of the market to satisfy the needs of businesses. Because this is exactly one of the failures of the market: not to recognise the needs of businesses unless monetarily expressed and to persist in undervaluing the social consequences of their actions.

4

BETWEEN THE DEREGULATING STATE AND THE REGIONAL NETWORKS: INDUSTRIAL DISTRICTS IN SPAIN

JUAN JOSÉ CASTILLO

Today it is universally recognised that Spain has the equivalent of Italy's Emilia-Romagna in the region surrounding Valencia, with its districts of localised manufacturing industries – for toys, wooden furniture, carpets, marble fashioning, ceramic crafts, shoemaking and so on. But it is not only this region that those who talk of the burgeoning of small firms have in mind. Navarre contains as many, in the field of alabaster or electronics, as does the Vallés region of Catalonia, covering a variety of activities. What seemed, early in the 1980s, to belong in the realm of – enclosed orders of nuns involved in data-processing for banks – has revealed itself as one truly original segment of small enterprise, that constituted by convents.

The fact that the (central) Ministry for Industry itself encouraged the decentralisation of industrial policy was, in 1992, a way of recognising that structures of production in Spain had so changed as to focus attention now on consituent regions and on their further development, on emphasising the local context in constructing the social fabric of the economy.

A recent industrial act promises to provide help with cooperation between firms, in particular between small and medium-size enterprises, for the sharing of, or joint demand for, services and the strengthening of associations and other appropriate bodies whose aim is to modernise and internationalise industry[1]. Again, in organising his campaign in 1992 – EXCEL (*Experiencia de cooperacion entre las empresas a nivel local*) – the Minister for Industry said that one of its aims was to 'propagate and promote local schemes for production insofar as they represent productive potential'.

In short, both in specialised publications and in mass circulation newspapers just as in political discussion, small firms today occupy a privileged and preeminent place. Yet the fact that the structure of production has undergone significant transformation does not necessarily imply division of labour between enterprises, where cooperation, trust, partnership and social dialogue prevail, on the lines of Marshallian industrial districts, merging reality with a plausible utopia.

Overall picture

According to the most reliable information available, small productive units multiplied spectacularly in Spain during the 1980s, and especially between 1985 and 1990, when their number rose from 688,000 to 1,100,000, an increase of almost 60 per cent. The 1990 figures are revealing: 53 per cent of wage-earners were in firms employing fewer than 50 people, 5 per cent more than in 1985; and 26 per cent, accounting for 2,200,000, in firms employing under 10 people.

Yet on closer examination this escalation needs to be qualified somewhat in order to allow for other forces of change in Spanish society. In the first place, firms consisting of a single person (i.e. self-employment) increased from 12,362 in 1985 to 173,069 in 1990. Second, the number of firms employing between 1 and 5 workers rose by 167,312. Within the same period, the yearly figure for business creation by 'wage-earning or self-employed entrepreneurs' remained at 75,000, advantage being taken of the expedient of capitalising unemployment benefit.

Recent studies show that length of unemployment is a greater factor in setting up a firm than any increase in entrepreneurial appetite *per se*. The earnings of those who are self-employed are 22 per cent lower than those of wage-earners whose profile is similar (Alba, 1992). Furthermore, legislation in 1984 concerning 'flexibility' in taking on labour and in further fiscal measures affecting the self-employed allowed some people to venture the notion that the underground economy was 'coming out into the open'. In other words, was a productive structure that previously had concrete existence now acquiring legal status?

On the other hand, measures that serve to encourage flexibility in the labour market oblige us to look at the context in which the reemergence, the 'comeback', of the small enterprise has been taking place. First of all, fixed-term, temporary contracts have increased spectacularly, so that whereas in the early 1980s they were insignificant, they now affect substantially more than a third of wage-earners. This insecurity leads workers to accept any type of employment. Further, temporary contracts are concentrated in small enterprises: every year nearly 90 per cent of employment contracts concern firms employing fewer than 50 wage-earners. If we take this in conjunction with the findings of surveys on employment where there is no contract or the rise in accidents at work, we may consider that working conditions bearing little resemblance to the pattern promoted by the welfare state are on the increase in small firms.

A further set of figures provides a backdrop to the Spanish labour market. In the course of the five-year period of growth – 1985–90 – a high level of unemployment developed, unrelated to that pertaining in adjacent countries. In 1986 it affected more than 20 per cent of the working population (i.e. 3 out of 14 million). If the figure fell now and then, the supply surplus remained above two million throughout the period, rising again markedly in 1993. This explains why surveys reveal a strong tendency to accept work that offers no guarantees and where no account is paid to qualifications gained, which is clearly a disadvantage to firms concerned with quality.

In these circumstances, the lack of negotiating strength among employees, their reduced purchasing power and the constraint upon them to accept working conditions hardly conducive to progress in their careers, act as a hindrance to the development of productivity by small firms. The necessary social preconditions are lacking.

Yet Industry thrives

Even so, if the different comprehensive or sector-based analyses clearly show there to be a general decrease in the size of firms, we know little about the links such firms may form with each other. On the other hand, there exist a number of well-documented regional or sector-based studies by which unusual ventures as well as industrial districts in the full sense of the term can be identified (Castillo, 1991).

The most recent assessment of the situation (Costa, 1992) is not strictly speaking a statistical analysis but a catalogue that constitutes a good representation of the problems, sectors and cross-firm dealings that face small firms. An examination was made of 23 areas and about 150 small enterprises, covering the treatment of marble (Macael, Andalusia); shipbuilding components (Vigo, Galicia); vegetable canning (Murcia); cheap jewellery (Minorca); foodstuffs (Guijuelo, Estremadura); car components (Madrid); machine tools (Bajo Eeba in the Basque country); and so on.

An area-by-area breakdown of the productive systems shows a clear distinction between:

● flexible systems or, properly speaking, industrial districts, with very close cooperative and competitive tie-ups among small enterprises. Such appears to be the case in the Onda-Alcora ceramics industry in the province of Castello (Valencia), the toy industry in Ibi (Allcante/Valencia) and software production in Sabadell (Catalonia):

● local productive systems built up round large firms 'set up in line with new organisational criteria', examples being Corredor de dos Hermanas in Andalusia, subcontracting for the aeronautical firm CASA, or at Martorell, a SEAT satellite.

In fact, too much haste in applying the term 'industrial district' to any form of localised production makes for confusion. Not all network types of production represent divisions of labour that are capable of undergoing development in the long term and modernising the form of production. Often it is not a case of 'flexible specialisation' for enterprises with a well-qualified labour force but of plan 'cost-cutting exercises' through flexible use of unskilled labour. One example of networks of this type may be mentioned before looking at the more dynamic local industrial networks – on the Valencia or Madrid model – which are also the most widespread (Sanchez, 1991–2). In Andalusia, these structures develop on parallel lines within the same region, independent of sophisticated technology, as in the aeronautical industry. Backing has been given to anarchic development, which is subject neither to norms, nor work contracts, nor respect for the environment, hence with highly negative consequences even if it does create employment in the short run. Barriers have been raised against technological, financial, commercial and production methods, resulting in inadequate services in firms, failure to coordinate public policies, and trade union exclusion. Such 'nebulous' industrial accumulations

(Bericat, 1990–1) have developed in the clothing industry where outworkers constitute the last link in a chain in which unskilled labour and poor pay prevail.

A real 'industrial district' worthy of the name should establish a division of labour between specialised firms enjoying a degree of autonomy and innovative capacity. At the same time it should develop a skilled workforce which can show initiative and be given a reasonable prospect of job stability across one or other of the firms forming a local labour market. It is always the case that certain firms coordinate others, but this is a different scenario from the simple division between a few head firms and a great number of anciliary ones, characterised by unskilled labour and poor working conditions.

Public policies

Finally, the new and growing role of public policies, and particularly of regional intervention policies, needs to be emphasised. Since 1985, even though some institutions were set up a few years earlier, there has been constant – sometimes overlapping – proliferation of regional development and intervention agencies which now cover virtually the whole of Spain.

Despite variation in levels of development and intervention methods that reflect differing political complexions and strategic goals, virtually all the self-governing regional communities in Spain now have a development agency, this being a consequence of the devolutionary policy followed since 1978, which in turn was reinforced when Spain joined the European Union, by European encouragement of regionalisation. The direction taken by such intervention and its recognisable repercussions depend on:

- regional policy, administrative rulings and the degree of commitment on the part of those who play a political or social role;
- strategic vision and planning in the administration of regional systems of production (Storper and Harrison, 1991);
- synergic integration of different policies – industrial and employment for example – consequent on the preceding point;
- concern to promulgate policies and give them the widest possible publicity with a view to incubating awareness of their real impact;

● the role given to social partners, interpreted in the widest sense, in formulating, applying and evaluating policies.

These policies serve to encourage 'collective order and economic coordination' (Scott and Paul, 1990), and engender a social consensus and a sense of identity that is seldom present at a regional level (Trigilia, 1991). To what extent do they channel multiple interests and boost confidence placed by the different social partners in the aims set?

In the absence of any authoritative comparative evaluation of these policies in different environments, one can only instance specific regional institutions which in a very short space of time have come to exert an extraordinary impact on the local economy. IMPIVA, set up in Valencia in 1984, has, among other things, contributed to the launching of a web of sector-based technological agencies, in ceramics, footwear, textiles, toys, etc., which have offered services to, and helped modernise industry. Since 1985 IMPIVA's budget has grown fourfold: between 1987 and 1991, firms having links with the technological agencies set up as 'associations for the corresponding sector' doubled in number; and – a significant statistic – 70 per cent of the 2,265 associated firms have fewer than 50 employees in their factories (Rico, 1992). The Valencia region, as has been said, presents the characteristics of a Spanish Emilia-Romagna.

It has given rise to a number of studies but as yet no comprehensive and up-to-date appraisal exists. The studies that are available draw attention to a mismatch between the interventionist projects and the real position of industry which shows a degree of reluctance to shift and change. Trade union assessments undertaken have called for a higher profile for those concerned with social issues (Sanchis *et al.*, 1989). The problem of getting through to industry and the slow progress of changes sought by public interventions are recurring features. Many of the agencies 'are unable to find enterprises to carry out their programmes' and acknowledge the distance that separates what they have to propose from its implementation.

In the Madrid region great changes have occurred since 1984 when the Madrid Institute for Development (IMADE) was set up. In 1986 a survey on 'new technologies in Madrid industry' gave a depressing view of the situation: more than half the firms made no call on the new technologies however broadly defined, and only 17.5 per cent of them had recourse to electronics. During the following three years more than half the plant was renewed, 'so allowing a very substantial increase in productive capacity and regional productivity'. Nevertheless the Institute discreetly admitted in 1992 that the number of innovative enterprises was 'genuinely limited' (IMADE, 1992: 3). Further, a detailed survey of one of the zones in the region, the Corredor del Henares, which accounts for more than a quarter of the industrial labour force, reveals that more than half the constituent firms – small and medium-size enterprises maintaining 'strong inter-firm relations' – are less than ten years old.

Certainly the Madrid scene is unrecognisable from what it was ten years ago. Now policy is orchestrated by the agencies together. Technological parks have been created, such as Alcala and Tres Cantos, the CAD centres, and a Madrid technology institute, Madrid-Laser. Negotiations have also been taking place, involving management and unions, to carry through a conception of development close to that of the industrial district. A good example of its operation is the Employment Plan put into effect by the combined action of industrial leaders, unions, municipalities and the regional government. Maybe there is still a long way to go in order to achieve what those responsible for policy emphatically call a 'new model for growth'. Yet it is clearly the case that the package of measures adopted add up to a 'different economic policy'. For example, a change occurred when in 1993 representatives of industry, unions, municipalities and the regional government signed a 'pact for industry and employment', which in its opening section declares: 'labour relations must move in the direction of cooperation, because the need to adapt to constant and crucial environmental changes demands a high degree of participation and commitment on the part of management and labour as regards planning, innovation and both training and organisation of the workforce'. Banking on social dialogue as a boost to production, a detailed series of industrial policy measures was drawn up, covering infrastructure, servicing, productivity and competitiveness. The President of the region himself asserted that such public policies would encourage 'cooperative links between firms, a necessary condition for innovation and competitiveness among small-sized enterprises, and work practice based on aptitude'.

Conclusion: both change and continuity

The radical changes that have taken place in Spain over the last fifteen years have affected small-scale firms no less than they have the economy and society as a whole. A complex process of social and economic transformation involving the restoration of democracy, membership of the European Union, and considerable reorganisation and readaptation has made its impact on conditions of work and production.

The years of growth, 1985 to 1990, were followed by a phase of recuperation from the recession in the first part of the 1980s, aggravated by the growing tension at national level resulting from inadequate negotiation over industrial policy during the last ten years. Spain has experienced two national strikes and several stoppages at regional level, evidence of the need for negotiation and a greater measure of participation.

A new means of articulating collective management of the economy so as to meet the challenge of the 1990s is emerging at regional level – in the self-governing communities of Madrid, Valencia, Catalonia, Castilla-Leon and Castilla-La Mancha, and Murcia. In the absence of national agreements regional industrial pacts are developing; and the disturbing news that unemployment has risen above the three million mark has prompted parliamentary debate.

Close to, on the ground, things take on greater clarity. The future strategy of small-scale enterprise systems calls for social dialogue and cooperation in deeds as well as in words. However, reality is one thing, aspiration another, and efforts foiled another again. The uncertainty of the labour market, which has reached a point one could hardly have envisaged ten years ago, provides a striking instance of the way in which the (highly) visible hand of industrial policies and the state of employment can create extremely negative conditions for the workforce. However, localised industrial zones and regional institutions involved in local networks of production constitute the other side of the district in difficult times such as these. It is then that a strategic vision is developed shaped by the local context and character of each area but directed or very strongly influenced by regional public policies. The visible hand, social dialogue and agreements attempt to make up for bad political habits. One is led to the conclusion that the outcome of the years ahead will depend in no small measure upon the policies actually implemented, which, in turn, will bring about very different solutions in Spain, hingeing not so much on the processes or products as on the actors.

5

DENMARK: MANY SMALL WORLDS

Peer Hull Kristensen

∞∞

Introduction

With its business structure persistently dominated by SMEs, Denmark might have been an experimental laboratory from which a new model of prosperity had emerged with the rise of the volatile economy by the mid-1970s. But unlike the Third Italy or Baden-Württemberg there have been no consistent signs that Denmark was waking and catching up to make creative use of a business structure that has proved favourable in other places.

Signs of Denmark's economic performance have been very mixed, indicating a welfare state in great trouble (high unemployment) and yet, recently, a picture is emerging of a strong economy, able to produce high trade surpluses and low inflation rates. Paradoxically this comes at a time when both the Third Italy and Baden-Württemberg are showing signs of trouble.

Few Danish observers see the indications of improvement as being due to a new dynamic within industry. Rather, the 'strong economy' is believed to be an effect of increasing personal savings, because during bad times the population prepares itself for an even worse situation. This radical break with traditional habits may indicate that Danes have adapted a 'subsistence survival strategy' (Sabel, 1993).

Yet industrial change seems very dynamic. Though aggregated national statistics show a remarkable stability of Danish industrial structure, considerable restructuring is taking place. Again the picture is mixed. Two very different dynamics have been at work simultaneously:

1. Dramatic de-industrialization in the eastern aisles of Denmark, primarily in Copenhagen.
2. Dramatic growth of industry in small towns of the agricultural districts of western Jutland.

This process has been accompanied by a new wave of mergers, as in many other countries, but the fast-growing counties in Jutland have primarily been based on the growth in number and employment of small independent firms. The last decade has been marked by fluctuations in economic activity in every region. However, regression lines through these ups and downs from 1982 to 1992 reveal a significant picture: unemployment is rising in the east, while in some counties of Jutland employment levels have improved. Two very different versions of Denmark have slowly evolved from a fairly even distribution of unemployment at the beginning of the 1980s. The strong and the weak parts can both be studied.

Regional differences within a country are part of the very discussion of new successful industrial districts of SMEs. However, in Denmark they are more difficult to explain than in Italy. In Denmark institutions supporting enterprises seem to be much more coherently organised at national level, access to supportive services seems to be less 'selectively' distributed and their location should have favoured firms in areas of de-industrialisation. Unions and employers are organised according to trades at a national rather than at a regional level, whereas in Italy unions and employers' organisations operating at the local level are able to help an industrial policy to be formulated and to develop strategies towards the region in question. A particularly good example is, of course, how CNA operates in Emilia.

This has two effects. On the one hand, the formation of interest groups operates on a national level and is thus rather at a disadvantage for developing new industrial publics at a regional level. On the other hand, as these interest groups need to integrate views which differ greatly between two very different situations, their role has rather been to create confusion.

In such a process, learning from a societal point of view is blocked. On the one hand, we have strong indications of an intensive process of experimentation going on within Danish industry, but we have few signs of this process being monitored and guided by discursive reflections. On the other hand, we have a political debate inspired, so it seems, by a great ability to pick up any idea from the international discourse on industrial organization, producing the reflections that in comparison with this or that Denmark's industry needs to be cured. Consequently, our theoretical reflection is disintegrated from our praxis.

Today such a disintegration between politics and the economy may be the rule in most countries. However, in Denmark this divide is more destructive than in most other countries because the Danish economy lacks integrative mechanisms. There is no easy solution to this problem when the formation of interest groups of the corporatist state holds the social space in which discourses of integration could take place, and uses this social space rather for producing disintegration.

In this chapter we set out to explain why Denmark on the one hand embodies a great ability to reproduce SMEs and, on the other, lacks integrative mechanisms that could help to evolve a 'system'. Then we try to show that such mechanisms may have been created in some places in Jutland. In analysing these, we point out some mechanisms that are of more than local interest. Finally we argue why such mechanisms have not been created on a national scale. We believe the diffusion of such mechanisms to be what is missing in turning Denmark into a coherent laboratory from which to learn the possibilities of prosperity.

Danish manufacturing industry – a non-system?

The standard solution to problems of disintegration in most market economies has been for large financial groups to take control and force firms into a corporate system of vertical and horizontal regulation. In most cases this has meant the destruction of an SME economy and the rise of large corporations.

Although strong powers tried to do the same in Denmark, it was the farmers who actually integrated the economy from 1870 to 1920. Their cooperative movement proved to be able to organise a self-contained value chain, controlling directly or indirectly such a large segment of the economy that they were able to coordinate exports of high quality butter, eggs and pork to rich countries (Kristensen and Sabel, 1993). The power of private financial groups became restricted and mainly played a role in Copenhagen and on Zealand.

Apart from being able to coordinate a large and complex system based on small producers (individual farms, local dairies, slaughterhouses), this whole complex also helped to develop and integrate a large sector of manufacturing SMEs into a very prosperous dynamic. Engaged in competition on foreign high-quality markets, the farmers' cooperative movement had to innovate continuously and in doing so they created a market at home for advanced methods in production, transportation, storage, selling and handling foodstuffs. Improvements in one link of the chain created new demands in another, and there were institutions to ensure that this incremental learning and improvement was monitored throughout the entire system.

This had the effect that a particular successful industry, mainly based on SMEs, emerged in such branches as food-processing equipment, freezing equipment, fast vessels and marine engines. Second, the machine-industry found a particularly high demand for small motors, and small electrical generators to serve the modernisation of small producers both within agriculture and industry. Denmark institutionalised very early the application of modern machines to small-scale uses. Instruments of all sorts to assist the control of quality in a very long value chain of agricultural processes created another demand for a very varied range of products. Finally, as the farmers lived in decentralised agricultural districts from which the initiative for cooperatives stemmed, the general pattern was to create small towns in which the local cooperatives grouped together, often close to a railway station. Such 'service centres' were ideal for craftsmen looking for opportunities to settle down as self-employed. Consequently, the agricultural areas became comparatively densely populated in Denmark and were composed of yeomen producers, representing a rich variety of technical skills, enabling these small communities continuously to modernise in most aspects of life. Many craftsmen started by providing local services, repairing, installing new equipment or constructing buildings at the local markets. Then gradually some evolved into shops producing products which were sold more widely on the national market, that they could reach through a very fine-meshed network of railways.

Copenhagen resembled much more closely the usual image of industrialisation. Larger factories, many in process industries, others in high-volume consumer products, developed here at a fast rate to produce the normal picture at that time of over-populated cities. But the general prosperity of the country, mainly produced by the success of the farmers, had effects here too. First, as the population had the choice of seeking employment in the country side, proletarisation was less widespread compared with large cities of other countries. Second, Danish unions soon learned that they could succeed by organising workers along the principles of the old craft guild system. Consequently, strong craft-based unions were able to influence the process of industrialisation.

For these reasons, within many trades (e.g. machine building, furniture making) it was possible to avoid 'sweating', with the unions forcing employers to look for the high quality end of markets, where domestic demand helped to pay for innovation or quality. In effect, large segments of manufacturing industry were dominated by SMEs making high-quality products.

Thus, though dominated to a remarkable extent by small businesses, the farmers cooperative export success created a very well-integrated economic dynamic that made Denmark one of the richest countries of the world by the 1920s. Compared with its situation a hundred years earlier, the transformation had been more impressive in terms of affluence than in any other European country and comparative wealth was very evenly distributed.

This road to industrialisation never depended on protectionism, as Danish farmers strongly believed that imports should help to cut costs in order to improve exports. In effect, Danish industrial prosperity owed itself to the relatively few areas where national demand was peculiar or skills and productivity were superior. Selecting these fields of specialisation did not take place without pain and struggle. In 1862 a law granted Danes the right to choose any occupation they wished, abolishing guild regulations. For a long period the craft guilds fought to have the old regulatory regime reinstalled. Then in the 1890s they tried to copy many of the institutions that made the farmers' cooperatives so successful. But their success with these two strategies was very limited. Rather than being able to use their associations to regulate competition, competition among craftsmen took place within them and left the crafts without monitoring capacities.

However, aided by past experience and supported by enlightened state administrations aggressive vocational training gradually emerged as the strategy that could solve the troubles of the Danish 'Mittelstand'. First, it found support from the craft unions, which saw vocational training and formalised apprentice contracts as a way of regulating the number within crafts. Second, it was seen by the craft associations as a means to compete with factory production – domestic or foreign – through quality production. Third, seeing vocational training as a means of introducing the most advanced methods of production, the crafts organised the first attempts to secure the transfer of new technologies. The system was initially developed in Copenhagen from schools covering a variety of disciplines. There then followed specialised schools for specific crafts set up to make the final courses and certification of journeymen. Schools for initial training were set up in many larger cities throughout the country, finally reaching the agricultural districts where technical schools were added to other institutions in the tiny railway towns. Although often initiated by local crafts-men, these local schools were from the outset part of a national system regulated by negotiations between craft associations, the state, teachers' associations and craft unions. On top of this system, schools for a range of engineering education for craftsmen were later developed, and a Technological Institute ensured that the entire complex was systematically renewed by transferring new technologies into courses, curricula and new 'crafts'. By 1907, when the last pieces of the complex were formally institution-alised, there existed a very self-conscious and modern perspective on the role of crafts, aimed at the creation of a decentralised indus-try, as was already the case with agriculture.

In many fields mass production was put to a competitive test by craftsmen trying to develop high-quality variants aided by their vocational institutions. In most cases this competitive test helped crafts to identify niches in which they could operate with small-scale production. In some areas they won the fight over a whole branch, as in furniture production and instruments. In the engi-neering and metalworking industries a widespread number of different crafts helped to define new industries. Factories within this branch were often large because they needed to combine a complicated number of craft workshops in order to make their products, which were generally produced for specific customers to their specific requirements. In some branches mass production eliminated the crafts and machines and unskilled workers took their place. However, compared to most other countries, mass production played a minor role in Denmark's industrial develop-ment.

Consequently, a large number, of Denmark's manufacturing establishments, of whatever size, were flexibly combining skilled workers with general-purpose machinery. In many cases, by being host to a large number of specialised craft shops, a large factory looked very much like a tiny railway town, which in the same manner contained a number of shops representing a wide scale of different crafts. The large factories developed in size because they produced complicated constructions (dairies, ships, marine engines, freezing equipment, while the small factories concentrated on a local market and specialised in a limited range of processes. Both were well adapted to follow the dynamics of the farmers' export adventure and its continuously shifting needs. Workers, on the other hand, were very mobile as the vocational training system and national craft unions made it easy to take new jobs outside their original locality. The young journeymen's tradition of travelling was maintained as a habitual pattern for seeking further training, with young men being employed in a number of firms before settling down in a specific locality, either as self-employed, journeymen or foremen in firms. Not only was this a remarkable system for spreading knowledge from one firm to another, it also helped to establish personal relations across hierarchies within organisations and across firms within a branch. If things needed to be coordinated with outside firms, most firms could easily tap their personal friends to make a cooperative effort possible. This probably explains why no serious efforts were ever made to make trade associations work as effective monitoring devices for developing cooperation.

Therefore, by 1920 Denmark possessed a remarkable systemic economy. Personal ties throughout industry and involvement in agricultural dynamics created the integration necessary to make the smallholder economy flourish. This system changed dramatically, though gradually, between 1925 and 1945. The carefully constructed export engine of the Danish farmers lost its dynamics as it became difficult to export and foreign producers had no free access to the Danish market with their products. The protectionism of the 1930s was especially harmful as it victimised both agriculture and firms which through specialization had been able to export niche products on the world market. However, the inherent flexibility of crafts and industries proved itself during these years. Large production plants used their resources for domestic demand, (e.g. shipyards producing bridges and heating systems). Small firms took to producing products that had usually been imported.

The small craft shops of Jutland's railway towns proved to be exceptionally advantageous. To compensate for seasonal fluctuations in activity they had often been engaged in some form of batch production, during winter. Now they simply extended this 'winter season' and as it was much easier to find workers in their localities, they gradually shifted from their normal local activities to 'factory' production for the larger national market. Many of Denmark's most well-known firms owe their initiation to this period and the phenomenon was so widespread that during the 1930s Denmark experienced its highest growth in manufacturing output. The main reason for this was SMEs in the agricultural service centres/railway towns of Jutland. While this period in many other countries was marked by the establishment of national monopolies or oligopolistic structures, in Denmark it meant a revitalisation of SMEs.

Before World War II Denmark's manufacturing industry was thus very fragmented but also very heterogeneous, while in many other countries a much more integrated, mass-producing economy had emerged and was to be reinforced during and after the war. For these reasons Denmark's industrial development from 1945 to 1965 is a story of many small worlds rather than one integrated logic. Though agriculture continued to play an important role, it had lost its capacity to set the dynamics nationally and locally, and yet it was capable of helping the Danish engineering industry to hold a strong position in agricultural machinery, food-processing equipment and instruments of measurement. Some producers of professional equipment were able to take advantage of expanded mass markets for consumer durables to become small domestic 'mass-producers'. Many of the SMEs created in the former period gradually left the arena as their owners aged, while others specialised in some sort of production in which craft knowledge paid off (furniture for the American market). Manufacturing industry gradually became the dominating economic activity in Denmark, but without establishing a clear structure as was the case in many other Western countries. No product or firm became dominant as, for example, cars in Sweden or consumer electronics in the Netherlands. Neither were SMEs just a part of a dual system, sweating for large producers, nor was a system of 'industrial districts' evolving as in Italy, except in some rare instances (Kristensen, 1992b). There were waves of mergers, but they helped to stabilise a fragmented industry rather than to structure it into a system (Kristensen, 1992a).

At the beginning of the 1970s it was easier to see what Denmark had specialised away from than what it had chosen. Standardised components, intermediate goods, consumer products and machinery (Kjeldsen–Kragh, 1973) had gradually been left, and leading industrialists were conscious that the guiding principle for strategy was to choose those niches in which world demand was so limited that large foreign corporations would ignore them.

Part of the story of Japan, the Third Italy and Baden–Württemberg is how it is possible to organise a 'product chain' across many firms instead of duplicating the American integrated corporation. With regard to Danish development, its industry was hardly able to construct one single value chain domestically. Rather firms were small nodes, related much more intensively – quantitatively speaking – to international producers and customers than to each other.

Our knowledge about how small Danish enterprises organised these international relations from the mid-1960s and later is limited. At that time they were operating in a sellers' market in which it was fairly difficult, especially for SMEs, to buy components when they were needed. It is also difficult to understand how small producers, predominantly skill-based manufactures of niche products, primarily offering for sale their skills and specialised processes, have been able to create one of the most export intensive national economies of the Western world.

Judged from the standard cycles of internationalisation (Forsgren and Johanson, 1975) Denmark's international relations can be classified as immature (Strandskov, 1987), as forward linkages to the international markets are predominantly organised through agencies. However, many Danish SMEs in manufacturing industry act simultaneously as agencies for one or several foreign firms. What they bring to the Danish market are often more standardised versions of products, which they make more customised, or components which are needed in their own products. Many foreign firms probably choose to let Danish firms act as agencies due to the small size of the Danish market.

This method of organising international relations much resembles the former way of the small craftshops in the railway towns. First, holding an agency helps such firms to stabilise turnover and incomes. If forced to reduce manufacturing activities in regard to niche products they are still active through their relations with local and national firms. Thus, each individual firm in a location relates to a complex network of regional, national and international firms. Even if a producer for the final market subcontracts some activities to a regional subcontractor, this subcontractor again organises deliveries by ordering supplies from regional, national and international sources. In return, producers of final products, whether capital equipment or producer goods, are, so to speak, linking the subcontractors with the final market, whether local, national or international (Grøn, 1985:94–101).

Though the coherence of 'value chains' is very limited indeed in the Danish case, firms are mutually able to help each other to be related to shifting partners of the international scene by choosing a limited number of Danish cooperators. The backward and forward linkages of the individual small firm towards regional, national and international relations is probably much more heterogeneous than in both the Japanese and Italian systems. Whereas in these systems the SMEs act as subcontractors in quite stable 'value chains', the nature of relations between firms helps each individual firm to be tied up in a large number of shifting value chains. So although coherence and integration of firms quantitatively may be low, we suggest that individual independent enterprises in a Danish location are far from being 'institutionally isolated' as Lane (1992) has shown the British SMEs to be.

Such a multiplication of the firms' own network by indirect ties helps to organise a much wider one than would be possible for the individual company. From a systems point of view, the firm continuously participates in a whole range of 'value chains' by applying its specialised assets flexibly to different customers. The risk of developing a niche strategy into a blind alley becomes less dangerous, but the other side of the coin is that it becomes very difficult to imagine a monitoring system which could integrate SMEs into systemic development.

International relations seem to be built on some stability, as holding agencies for each other introduces an element of reciprocity, so that it is possible to imagine forms of cooperative monitoring. Relations with other Danish firms seem essentially to be based on the mobility nationally of persons belonging to different crafts and professions. It is through this mobility – vertical and horizontal – that they become members of a community of practitioners within segments of industrial branches.

As argued elsewhere (Kristensen 1992a, b), the Danish labour market is strongly influenced by a craft organisation, which regulates the labour market on a national scale. As a result of this the horizontal mobility of skilled workers is possible on a national scale, whether an apprentice has started his career in a small rural village or in Copenhagen. For these reasons, many entrepreneurs, managers or middle managers of SMEs, among whom there is a strong dominance of people with a journeyman background (Maskell, 1992:255), have had jobs in many locations and established relations with colleagues and entrepreneurs in many places. Especially when sons are preparing to take over their father's SME, a period of extensive training combining several degrees of vocational training with many different job experiences on top of an apprentice period can be very formative for their ability to relate their business to a larger context than the locality (see Kristensen, 1992b: 153). Needless to say, by experiencing different jobs in different firms, gradually climbing from a skilled worker to higher positions, is also a way of getting to know how different firms relate to regional, national and foreign firms. Such experience of methods of doing business in a specific branch seems to be decisive for a new entrepreneur and one of the most important factors determining whether a new firm will succeed or fail (Maskell, 1992:189 cont.).

In short, building up job experience is also a way of connecting to other enterprises, and as careers at work may bring a skilled worker to different localities before he starts his own business or achieves a management position, neither the local labour market nor the local industrial structure in Denmark seems to create the tight social ties which have been said to be so important for understanding the organisation of the Italian industrial district. In conclusion, nothing seems to work in favour of integrating SMEs at a local level in Denmark.

The creation of industrial districts

Since the beginning of the 1970s the tendency of manufacturing industry has been to agglomerate. The successful localities owe their prosperity to the fact that they are building up employment within a specialised branch: 'Most favoured are regions dominated by a single manufacturing sector or which are dominated by a single, large manufacturing firm, thus representing a high degree of local specialization' (Maskell, 1992: 311).

The birth of this new pattern happened through a volatile process. More than half of all the incumbent manufacturing firms which existed in 1972 were closed by 1988 (Maskell, 1992: 310). During this process Denmark has been transformed into many small worlds. A combination of relatively few company closures, increasing employment in existing firms and the formation of new ones in peripheral/agricultural regions, primarily in West Jutland where the population of the largest town accounted for a maximum of 5,000 people, have been able to compensate for the decline, which happened mainly in larger towns, primarily in the eastern part of the country and primarily in Copenhagen. The result has been a vast 'relocation' of industry.

This important spatial regrouping is only to a negligible degree the effect of relocated establishment of firms formerly located in the eastern part of the country. Most new and old firms owe their existence to local entrepreneurs and such entrepreneurial activity seems to be especially intensive in small communities in the western part of Denmark, while it is fairly low in the eastern part of the country, even in communities of the same size and similarly located in a primarily agricultural area. Furthermore, new firms seem to survive better in the west than in the east. So while western Jutland seems gradually to develop a pattern of industrialisation similar to the Third Italy, the eastern agricultural areas and their towns tend to lose the industrial settings that used to be there.

While it is difficult to explain these disparities by differences in institutions or networks among firms, it is not difficult to identify differences in history and traditions. In the eastern region agriculture was organised through large estates making use of agricultural labourers, while in Jutland independent farmers and smallholders dominated the population. Thus, while in the east the transformation from agricultural labourer to smallholder was often associated with entrance into a social vacuum, in Jutland such a transformation was considered tantamount to be becoming a free 'man'. While in Jutland many institutions – local saving banks, schools, etc. – were seen as instruments to assist individuals in this transformation, in the east they were often managed by estate owners and the higher circles to protect the lower classes against their own failures – and the patrons against increasing tax burdens. Thus, while class divisions were very clear in the east, in the west different class positions were rather stations of life, where agricultural workers would change their situation from working for different employers over the year to doing part-time farming on their small lots, eventually increasing these lots in order to be able to live as small independent farmers (Dammgaard, 1983). While members of communities in the west shared the experience of difficulties involved in such careers and were able to help each other, in the east few knew about these troubles and only patrons possessed the economic means to help.

In Jutland this career pattern altered only marginally when a larger proportion of these communities started to look for a craft career after World War II. Careers now changed to apprentice, journeyman and then master, but it was a road towards the same independence as in agriculture. Often craftsmen from agricultural families inherited the necessary funds to set up a small shop in a railway town. In the east neither tradition nor capital made it easy to look for a self-employed career. Most often, agricultural workers would look for unskilled jobs in local industries or move to a large town, often to Copenhagen.

This transformation was easy in Jutland because the railway towns already possessed an abundance of craft shops ready to receive new apprentices. Signing an apprentice contract provided more than a poorly paid job. It opened the door to a fully developed national community of craftsmen, vocational training facilities and services ready to help realise exactly the career pattern required. One of the major reasons why Jutland's new industrialisation has not resulted in a wave of new associations of employers is that a well-functioning system is already in existence.

A closer look into some of the industrialising regions in Jutland shows, however, that they did not just passively adjust themselves to this system, rather they made social use of these institutions to help their locality and industry fight for a space within Danish society. Significant institutions of the Danish welfare state were in this way actively adjusted to the yeoman republics of Jutland (Kristensen, 1992b, c; 1993a, b).

Reforms of the vocational training system have occurred continuously with varying intensity. These were most often made from a national point of view, negotiated in tripartite commissions within the state. The idea was to create a standardised national coherent system. Observers during the 1960s could have interpreted the closing down of local schools and the creation of regional centres of vocational training specialities, open to apprentices from the whole country, as centralisation of the entire system.

No doubt it had this effect on some regional centres. Today, however, it appears that in some active regions this process of centralisation created an opportunity to act and to build a regionally oriented training system. One example (see Kristensen 1992b) is the creation of a local complex of schools and technological institutes in Herning-Ikast garment 'district'. Gradually these institutions and the regional SMEs have interacted in such a way that a self-reinforcing process has been established. A finely structured vocational system makes it easy for workers gradually to improve their education, shifting between jobs and vocational modules, so that personal careers are almost moulded into the life pattern of craftsmen. The same phenomenon can be observed in Salling, where the technical schools and the AMU-centres in Skive have gradually created a similar system of education covering the simplest training of woodworkers, a range of specialised craft education with cabinetmakers, further training for advanced machinery and new technology and on top of this education for managers of furniture factories. In these two examples the concentration of institutions of a certain orientation within a region has not surprisingly, implied an over-concentration of specific skills that only need the already mentioned tradition for self-employment in Jutland to lead to an agglomeration of specific manufacturing sectors. Since 1955 such communities have transformed themselves from agricultural to industrial areas, with a proportion of skilled workers no less than the former industrial cities.

Within the lifetime of an individual entrepreneur some of these firms, which in the 1920s operated like local smallholder craftsmen, have been transformed into high-quality producers, some even having their products on permanent display in foreign museums of modern art. Yet some of their basic recipes for economic behaviour essentially resemble the logic by which their ancestors developed their small lots as smallholders in the old agricultural communities (Kristensen, 1992b).

Thus, the very creation of these firms is based on the philosophy of flexibility. As smallholders looking for shifting employment through the year, these firms were accustomed to combining a variety of activities over seasonal fluctuations. With the decrease in agricultural employment, they got a larger supply of skilled workers and stabilised by producing different products over the year. Workers and machines were flexible and they managed these resources more from the philosophy of a household accountant than from aspirations of growth and quick profits.

The rise of the volatile economy and the rapid decline in mass production did not call for major changes in this behaviour, but it had a great impact on the tendency to agglomerate certain sectors of industry in specific localities. While textiles in Herning and furniture in Salling proved successful from 1973 to 1993, other SMEs were in trouble. One of the most crisis-ridden sectors has been the building and construction industry. Many cabinetmakers, for example, have had to ask their neighbours in the furniture industry for 'help' in starting to do subcontracting for their more lucky neighbours. In effect the crisis has been a source of multiplying these local systems with an increasing number of independent units. But just as the smallholder wished to become independent of the help from his neighbours, the ambition of these small furniture makers is to show that they can do business on their own and be able to pay back their debt to their neighbours. Thus a newly created subcontractor looks for any opportunity to find his own product and his own customers, thereby breaking out of a pattern that could integrate the local system into a more coherent value chain.

During the 1980s a volatile economy presented itself to these business communities as a combination of high unemployment together with a lack of skilled workers, high interest rates, new technologies and rapid changes in currency values among their export markets. The universal answer to these challenges has been further training, and employees in Jutland have used the institutional possibilities of further training much more intensively than in any other part of Denmark. To reduce interest payments firms tried to reduce stocks and in order to reduce stocks they reorganised production into teams, responsible for a defined range of products and for reducing throughput time, thus enabling them to adopt just-in-time methods. The establishment of the teams on new computer-based work stations allowed the individual workplace to shift quickly from one product or variant to another. The implication was that the individual workers would integrate planning and execution. In consequence the demand rose greatly for further training of skilled and specialised workers. One aspect was that workers should be specialists in their narrow fields and be able to use new production equipment quickly; another was that in order to do a proper job in their individual workspace they should be able to understand it as part of a larger process. Finally they needed to be able to respond to wishes from customers or instructions and manuals written in foreign languages. The pressure on the individual employee increased dramatically. In regions that had gradually built a complex of vocational institutions this challenge initiated a new change in the pattern of further training. Formerly a journeyman who went for specific further education as *teknikum* engineer (lasting three-and-a-half years) or as a foreman dominated the pattern. A number of causes affected the decline of this system. First, whereas originally only journeymen could embark on such an education, from the late 1960s the *teknikum* engineer education became increasingly dominated by high-school students and manufacturing industry gradually lost interest in such engineers. Second, with the increasing tendency of workers to buy their own house in their youth, personal reasons often kept people from undertaking a new distinct phase of education.

Gradually, but with increasing intensity, regional clusters of schools (commercial technical, AMU centres and adult education centres) engaged in developing short courses of further training. Consequently, workers and white-collar employees have tended to adopt a new pattern in which they keep their job continuously and attend shorter courses of further training. For a long time courses of further training were rather specialized, oriented towards specific functions within firms and related to the groups which different types of schools saw as their specific clients. But in some regions today a new pattern is emerging. Schools cooperate in shifting roles as subcontractors and main contractors to develop entirely new curricula in which they match their capabilities in an endless number of combinations by which they can tailor courses to meet the needs of the local business community and the workers. In short, in some regions people have discovered that they possess a means of infinite training opportunities, which may be managed as a Benetton system of further training (Kristensen, 1993b).

The potential effects of this changing pattern may be impressive. Consider first the internal organisation of manufacturing firms. Formerly, the journeymen made the distinct leap in their careers by taking a longer education at a distant school and becoming middle managers. In doing so they were separated in two ways from the ongoing group life of their former colleagues. Today, journeymen become 'managers' as, by holding different jobs and attending different courses over time, they become so experienced that they are able to understand the organisation or industry in which they work cross-sectionally or cross-functionally. But they are now rather a part of ongoing group life among workers, who share almost the same development in skills and experience. The difference between the two groups – managers and workers – has narrowed and is often very difficult to specify.

Second, consider the relations among firms in a region. Where formerly *teknikum* engineers and foremen as well as commercially educated white-collar workers obtained their education in places far from their home region, naturally creating personal relations which tended to disperse their contacts over the entire country, today this situation may be changing. Although local further training courses are in most cases open to the entire country, it is likely that during a series of courses people from the same locality will meet each other more frequently than will happen cross-regionally. At the same time this network building now happens in a

more widespread way across the layers of the individual organisation, so that the firm becomes entangled in a much more varied
system of personal networks than used to be the case when access
to training was less evenly distributed between top and bottom.
Consequently, workers and managers may develop a personally
rooted network that relates the firm on many levels to other firms
in the region.

Through these mechanisms a CNC worker may be totally
informed about which firms have which CNC machines in the
region, knowledge that may be important for him when looking
for a new job, but may also be important for the firm where he
holds his present job. On the one hand, it urges him to press for
new investment by his firm so that he may remain confident that
his skills are not becoming obsolete because the firm is using old-
fashioned technology. On the other hand, this knowledge is very
important for the firm, if it suddenly discovers that it needs a
specific form of processing in order to be able to serve a customer
better at short notice. So though the quantitative subcontracting
relations may be weak, the person-bound relations between firms
may be very intensive indeed, and especially make it possible to
each resort to the other in times of trouble, when there is a need
to act swiftly. We imagine that through these mechanisms a
community of practitioners is being created that relates firms at
many levels, making it possible to cooperate in spite of a seemingly
very fragmented business community.

One of the most revealing cases we have studied is the local
subsidiary of a large Copenhagen bank (Høpner-Petersen, 1992).
During the last five or six years this bank has been eagerly trying
to integrate the subsidiaries created from the merger of three
large banks in the late 1980s. One means adopted has been to
design a large, detailed and standardized internal training system.
We expected these mechanisms to improve the financial expertise
of the local branch office but at the same time to make it isolated
locally, gradually destroying the detailed and specific knowledge
such as a branch office needs in order to reduce risks. It is quite
easy to imagine a vicious circle from the local point of view. But
the local branch office had found a way out of its troubles. First,
as bank assistants feared that they could not depend on a job in
the financial sector, they had eagerly engaged in further training
at local schools in order to improve their mobility on the local
labour market. By doing so they were engaged in the processes of
local integration as sketched out above. Consequently, the local

bank office continuously developed personal ties between the business community and its employees. Furthermore by working as bank advisers in teams they have gradually developed an internal division of responsibility, so that they specialise individually and then teach each other about specific areas and specific industries. Although the knowledge of these teams must be broad, this allows them to develop specific knowledge of certain branches. A very helpful means is to attend specialized further training courses for specific groups in order to understand how they work, how they think and where they see trouble in their business. Finally, the manager was very much in favour of such initiatives, as it made it easier to cut losses and increase earnings at the local branch. Because of this the Copenhagen bank considered it to be very successful and allowed it quite high autonomy in managing its funds. A virtuous circle had indeed been established.

We have only sketched out how a system may thus emerge to allow a region of firms heavily engaged in national and international relations to enlarge constantly their ability to cooperate. We think, in Denmark, that such mechanisms of cooperation need to be very heterogeneous and it is exactly through the large selection of further training courses that a small though overlapping 'industrial public' may be able to deal with this variety.

Many small worlds

We have indicated that one reason for prosperous regions in Jutland may be that they have changed the social use of vocational training institutions in such a way that they not only make possible the radical modification of the internal organisation of firms, but also create the type of integration among them that makes it valuable for a fragmented business community to cooperate.

This process of transformation has neither been planned nor monitored from a central office and its actual success has hardly been recognized by observers from the business community or the political institutions. Its process of creation owes itself to experimental trial and error of a joint number of independent practitioners rather than to a reflective process of political or strategic discourse. For this reason it is quite obvious that such a new pattern may be found in some regions but not in others.

However, we think that there is reason to believe that such

processes of trial and error are less likely in the agricultural regions of east Denmark than they have been in Jutland. The business community and the body of politics in the east is much more dominated by the strategies of a leading group of top managers of externally owned enterprises and estate owners. These have been able to manage vocational schools much more coherently for their own ends, and experiments involving a larger segment of the population have been limited. In Jutland, so our findings indicate, firms, employees, unions and vocational institutions have engaged in strategic experimentation of a much more varied and uncoordinated type that paradoxically enables coordination.

This experimental route is dependent on schools' ability to trust that they have local support to engage in experiments which may be anticipated as 'near the line' from the perspective of central government. Firms must be willing to accept that workers on a broad scale gain knowledge, which make them more mobile on the labour market, while workers, on the other hand, must feel confident that their investment in further training is worthwhile. In the estate communities of the east, we believe that social cohesion has been less than in Jutland, primarily due to lack of tradition for owner-producers (smallholders and the self-employed). Consequently, in the estate communities, there is no space between the governing and governed classes, and it is exactly this space that is becoming densely populated both within and between industrial firms in Jutland.

Why then are not all traditional smallholder communities in Jutland developing a particular form of industrial districts? The process of transformation we have described is basically happening under conditions of trust. It is the dynamic that can happen when people and institutions operate within 'fede publica' (Pagden, 1988). But we have indicated no monitoring capacities that allow the reproduction of such 'fede publica'. On the contrary, as new firms are often initiated in the same branch and the same locality where the new entrepreneur used to be employed, trust is likely to be very fragile. If communities echo the interpretation of a newly created firm as an instance of imitation and unfair competition, such communities may gradually develop into 'gang-communities'. Firms associating themselves with others against another gang may create a situation in which it is almost impossible for vocational institutions, workers and political bodies to engage in experiments which may develop the pattern we have suggested. While firms seem to be without mutual regulatory bodies of their own, we think these community differences play a very important role, and as firms are operating within very different types of community, it is quite understandable that their industrial record differs dramatically. Any community in Denmark probably embodies a specific blend of the three ideal types we have mentioned so far (*'fede publica'*, 'gang community' and 'patron-client estates'). For this reason they share a fundamental problem: can trust be created or maintained? (Sabel, 1992).

6

WHY ARE THERE NO INDUSTRIAL DISTRICTS IN THE UNITED KINGDOM?

Jonathan Zeitlin

Small firms and industrial districts: another peculiarity of the British?

One of the few points of agreement in current debates on small and medium-sized enterprises is that there are no industrial districts in the United Kingdom. More specifically, despite the undeniable resurgence of small firms and self-employment during the 1970s and 1980s, close observers of the British scene have been unable to identify localised networks of small and medium-sized firms specialising in distinct phases of a common industrial sector, which also display evidence of economic dynamism and endogenous growth. Insofar as elements of such productive systems can be found in contemporary Britain, they are generally concentrated in declining sectors and regions, while economic linkages between local firms often appear to have become weaker rather than stronger in recent years.

What makes this absence of dynamic industrial districts in the UK noteworthy is, of course, the contrast with recent developments in other advanced economies. Despite the intense theoretical and empirical controversies with which this book is concerned, a strong case can be made that industrial districts or district-like phenomena have made a significant contribution over the past decade and a half to the performance of such relatively successful economies as Italy, Germany, Japan, Spain and Denmark. Even in countries where the re-regionalisation of production has been decidedly more limited, such as France, Sweden, Canada and the

USA, dynamic examples of industrial districts or analogous localised productive systems have nonetheless been convincingly identified (Sabel, 1989; Pyke and Sengenberger, 1992). Hence, at least at first glance, there does appear to be some prima facie justification for speaking of national peculiarities or British 'exceptionalism' in relation to wider international trends, and thus for posing the question: 'Why are there no industrial districts in the United Kingdom?'

But this allusion to Werner Sombart's famous question, 'Why is there no socialism in the United States?' (Sombart, 1976) should immediately give us pause. For the long debate over American exceptionalism spawned by Sombart's question – like the related controversy over the German *Sonderweg* or special path (Blackbourn and Eley, 1984) – richly illustrates the dangers of taking any stylised developmental trajectory as a universal norm against which particular national experiences are judged as deviant. For as more systematic comparative studies demonstrate, each national trajectory can be considered 'special', 'peculiar' or 'exceptional' in certain respects, whether the issue under consideration be the development of labour politics, the establishment of parliamentary democracy, or the evolution of industrial structure (Zolberg, 1986; Tolliday and Zeitlin, 1991).

Returning from such broad theoretical considerations to the narrower theme of industrial districts as such, there are more specific reasons to be wary of framing our analysis in terms of British exceptionalism. For as the chapters in this volume illustrate, there is no universally accepted definition or model of what constitutes an industrial district, while the multiplicity of cases subsumed under this rubric display wide variations in internal structure, social complexion and economic performance.

Even within the industrial districts of the 'Third Italy' itself, as Arnaldo Bagnasco points out in his introduction, the past decade has seen significant changes in the roles of formalised governance structures, organised groupings of firms and relations with external capital which call into question the 'canonical' model of the district as it was originally formulated by Italian observers such as Giacomo Becattini (Becattini, 1989, 1990) and Sebastiano Brusco (Brusco, 1982, 1986). At the same time, as Bagnasco also emphasises, large firms themselves have been decentralising, devolving and disintegrating their operations into looser networks of semi-autonomous subsidiaries, franchisees, subcontractors, joint ventures and strategic alliances.

Rather than signalling the imminent eclipse of the industrial district, however, such developments can be understood as part of what Charles Sabel has called the 'double convergence' of large and small firm structures, as small firms in the districts build wider forms of common services inspired by large firm models, while large firms seek to recreate among their subsidiaries and subcontractors the collaborative relationships characteristic of the districts. This process of double convergence has given rise in turn to a proliferation of hybrid forms of organisation which fall between the canonical models of the industrial district and the vertically integrated corporation, as well as a multiplication of more explicit alliances and exchanges between firms of both types (Sabel, 1989).

For all these reasons, I have argued elsewhere (Zeitlin, 1992), it seems necessary to move away from a 'thick', 'closed' model of the industrial district based on a stylised account of the Italian experience towards a 'thin', 'open' model capable of accommodating a variety of empirically observable forms. Such a model might take its point of departure from Alfred Marshall's original definition of the district as a geographically localised productive system based on an extended division of labour between small and medium-sized firms specialised in distinct phases of a common industrial sector (Marshall, 1922: 267–90; 1927: 283–8; 1975: 195–8; See also Bellandi, 1989). It also might draw on Brusco's notion of intermediate or hybrid cases defined in terms of their distance from this ideal type: for example, the degree of localisation, the size distribution of productive units, and the extent of inter-firm linkages (Brusco, 1992). But it would not assume that industrial districts so defined are necessarily innovative, flexible, consensual or otherwise successful, since stagnant or declining districts also display many of the same structural features, nor would it assume that as districts develop they will necessarily converge towards the pure model.

Alfred Marshall's Britain: an economy of industrial districts

From a more parochial national perspective, too, the question 'Why are there no industrial districts in the United Kingdom?' raises evident difficulties. For as my earlier reference to Alfred Marshall reminds us, the concept of the industrial district was originally developed by a British economist on the basis of contemporary British experience. Among the industrial districts discussed in Marshall's *Industry and Trade*, first written in 1919, figured such British examples as Lancashire cottons, Sheffield cutlery, and South Wales tinplate (Marshall, 1927: 283–8). But the term 'industrial district' was already a commonplace of British economic and social description, and many other localized industries of the period displayed similar characteristics to those discussed by Marshall. Examples of such localised industries documented by contemporary commentators, regional geographers and economic historians include: hardware, guns and cycles in Birmingham (Allen, 1929); pottery in North Staffordshire (Whipp, 1990); hosiery, knitwear and footwear in Nottingham and Leicester (Head, 1968; Wells, 1972); clothing, furniture, printing and footwear in London (Hall, 1961); furniture in High Wycombe (Oliver, 1966); woollens and worsteds in West Yorkshire and the Scottish borders (Jenkins and Ponting, 1982); and the 'silk triangle' of Macclesfield, Congleton and Leek (Pyke, 1987).

Most of these turn-of-the-century British districts concentrated on the production of consumer goods. But regional agglomerations were also significant in the production of capital goods such as iron and steel, machinery and ships on the north-east coast of England and in the west of Scotland (Tolliday, 1987: part I; Lorenz, 1991; Zeitlin, forthcoming), as well as motor vehicles and components in the west Midlands (Thoms and Donnelly, 1985), though enterprises were typically larger and inter-firm linkages less dense than in the consumer goods sector. If we include these capital goods-producing regions, then turn-of-the-century Britain can fairly be characterized as an economy dominated by industrial districts. Before World War I, in any case, large, autarchic and vertically integrated firms remained rare outside of a narrow range of sectors such as food, drink and tobacco; chemicals; rail transport; and gas lighting (Fitzgerald, 1987; Tolliday and Zeitlin, 1991: 279–82).

One possible response to this historical litany of British examples might be that they were not really 'industrial districts' in the same 'canonical' sense as those of the 'Third Italy'. Certainly these historical British districts did not generally emerge from a similar matrix of independent artisanry, share cropping and peasant proprietorship, or Socialist and Catholic political subcultures which nurtured their Italian counterparts (Trigilia, 1986; Bagnasco, 1988).[1]

It might also be objected that these British districts lacked the dense web of reciprocity and cooperation among local actors characteristic of the Third Italy. But leaving aside the vexed question of how far this idyllic picture of economic coordination through shared values really captures the forces at work in the Italian case, there is abundant evidence of cooperation in these British districts. During the eighteenth and early nineteenth centuries, for example, small firms in Birmingham hardware and West Yorkshire woollens created cooperative joint-stock smelting, fulling and scribbling mills to safeguard their access to raw materials, while Birmingham gunmakers established a proof house to certify the quality of locally produced firearms (Sabel and Zeitlin, 1985: 148–9). Most British districts also developed local employers' associations and technical schools or colleges to regulate the supply and price of skilled labour, while regional boards of conciliation and arbitration were widespread means for resolving disputes with the workforce (Tarling and Wilkinson, 1982; Pollard, 1989: ch. 3). Local technical societies and later cooperative research associations provided extensive opportunities for discussing common problems and pursuing joint solutions to them (Edwards, 1950; Varcoe, 1981; Zeitlin, forthcoming). One recent account of the way information sharing within such technical societies enabled firms on the northeast coast to improve blast-furnace design during the third quarter of the nineteenth century goes so far as to speak of a process of 'collective invention' (Allen, 1983).

Significant differences can undoubtedly be discerned between these historical British districts and their modern Italian counterparts – as for that matter between the Italian districts and those in other countries or even among the Italian districts themselves. But there seems little justification for denying the applicability of the term 'industrial district' to the former on the basis of a canonical model derived from the latter's experience. It would in any case be the height of perversity to argue that while Alfred Marshall invented the concept in turn-of-the-century Britain, its true empirical referent would only appear in Italy half a century later.

Why are there no longer industrial districts in the United Kingdom?

The progress of the argument so far suggests a significant reformulation of my original question from 'Why are there no industrial districts in the United Kingdom?' to 'Why are there no longer industrial districts in the United Kingdom?' A full answer to this reformulated question would obviously require a detailed historical reconstruction of the fates of the many British industrial districts enumerated earlier which is beyond the scope of a short essay. But a brief sketch of the chronology and causes of their decline will help to orient a discussion of the more recent British experience.

Some of these British districts had begun to lose their economic and technological dynamism for a variety of contingent reasons before 1914. Thus Sheffield cutlery, for example, lost ground to its German rival Solingen (also organised as a small-firm district) because of manufacturers' concentration on slowly growing quasi-luxury markets and failure to mechanise key stages of production, tendencies reinforced by the power of local craft unions seeking to preserve the existing division of labour. In Birmingham hardware, too, many metalworking shops responded to depressed demand for their products during the late nineteenth century by becoming subcontractors for large bicycle, motor vehicle, and electrical equipment firms, gradually losing their technical and commercial autonomy in the process. But as in the parallel case of France discussed by Bernard Ganne in Chapter 7, most British industrial districts survived with at least mixed success until after World War II.[2]

The decisive shift occurred between the late 1940s and the early 1970s, as the share of the 100 largest firms in manufacturing output leapt from 22 per cent in 1948 to 40 per cent in 1970, and thousands of smaller companies disappeared through mergers and takeovers. By 1968, as Table 6.1 shows, firms with fewer than 100 employees accounted for 11.5 per cent of output and 13.5 per cent of employment in UK manufacturing, while those with fewer than 500 employees accounted for 23.7 per cent of output and 27.7 per cent of employment. Despite problems of comparability across national statistics, these proportions were the lowest by a considerable margin among the major industrial economies at that time (Dunne and Hughes, 1990; Loveman and Sengenberger, 1990).

As in France, too, this process of concentration and restructuring was fostered by deliberate state policies which saw the creation of 'national champions' large enough to realise economies of scale as crucial to the technological modernisation of domestic industry (Hall, 1986: 51–6; Young with Lowe, 1974). But concentration policies as such were only part of the story. For many smaller firms, the institutional organisation and regulation of the capital

Table 6.1 Establishments enterprises and the shares of output and employment by employment size class: UK manufacturing 1963–86

Year	No. est.	% share Est.	% share Emp.	% share Out.	Size class 1–99 No. ent.	Size class 1–99 No. est.	Size class 1–99 P/E ratio	% share Ent.	% share Emp.	% share Out.	Total est employment 000s
1963	75675	84.2	20.2	17.6	58166	60868	1.1	88.7	14.0	11.8	1606
1968	77793	84.8	20.3	18.1	55234	58092	1.1	89.5	13.5	11.5	1586
1970	75041	85.4	18.4	16.4	69095	71385	1.0	91.1	15.8	13.9	1482
1979	96768	90.1	20.4	17.8	84229	88226	1.1	93.9	17.2	14.6	1419
1981	99303	91.7	24.0	21.1	85189	89797	1.1	94.7	20.3	17.1	1388
1983	94384	92.1	26.1	22.3	81474	85753	1.1	94.8	22.0	18.0	1327
1984	127219	93.9	27.1	22.8	114186	118352	1.0	95.8	23.4	18.8	1368
1986	137850	94.4	28.3	23.6	125503	129656	1.0	96.4	24.0	19.3	1381
					Size class 100–499						
1963	11487	12.8	30.7	28.6	5653	9781	1.7	8.6	15.6	13.4	2439
1968	11144	12.1	30.7	28.4	4967	8626	1.7	8.0	14.2	12.2	2399
1970	10019	11.4	27.0	25.7	5136	7003	1.4	6.8	13.9	12.7	2171
1979	8284	7.7	25.6	25.0	4152	6804	1.6	4.6	12.9	11.6	1762
1981	7092	6.5	26.0	25.0	3601	6522	1.8	4.0	13.4	12.2	1505
1983	6424	6.3	27.0	25.8	3369	6112	1.8	3.9	14.4	11.6	1372
1984	6714	5.0	28.1	27.1	3904	6796	1.7	3.3	16.5	14.9	1420
1986	6617	4.5	28.8	27.9	3688	6778	1.8	2.8	15.9	14.5	1407
					Size class 500–999						
1963	1637	1.8	14.2	14.8	821	2935	3.6	1.3	7.7	7.4	1132
1968	1653	1.8	14.6	15.1	711	2556	3.6	1.2	6.8	6.4	1139
1970	1609	1.8	13.9	14.4	741	1949	2.6	1.0	6.8	6.7	1116
1979	1318	1.2	13.1	13.6	609	2170	3.6	0.7	6.6	6.8	911
1981	1105	1.0	13.2	13.8	560	2291	4.1	0.6	7.2	7.3	761
1983	993	1.0	13.3	14.2	530	1964	3.7	0.6	7.5	7.7	676
1984	966	0.7	13.1	13.9	524	1779	3.4	0.4	7.4	7.1	661
1986	645	0.6	13.2	13.7	508	1787	3.5	0.4	7.4	7.2	643
					Size class 1000+						
1963	1187	1.3	34.9	39.0	953	11163	11.7	1.5	62.7	67.3	2775
1968	1198	1.3	34.5	38.3	833	13069	15.7	1.3	65.5	69.8	2702
1970	1233	1.4	40.6	43.5	850	9052	10.7	1.1	63.5	66.7	3264
1979	1023	0.9	40.9	43.6	751	9876	13.2	0.8	63.0	67.0	2832
1981	776	0.7	36.8	40.1	627	9353	14.9	0.7	59.0	63.4	2124
1983	644	0.6	33.5	37.7	544	8344	15.3	0.6	56.0	61.4	1704
1984	623	0.5	31.8	36.2	558	7191	12.9	0.5	52.7	59.0	1610
1986	577	0.4	29.7	34.8	544	7631	14.0	0.4	52.8	59.1	1447
					All manufacturing						
1963	89896				65593	84747	1.29				7952
1968	91788				61745	82343	1.33				7826
1970	87902				75822	89589	1.18				8033
1979	107393				89741	107076	1.05				8926
1981	108276				89977	107963	1.20				5778
1983	102445				85917	102173	1.19				5079
1984	135522				119172	134148	1.13				5059
1986	145989				130243	145852	1.12				4878

Sources: Census of Production Historical Statistics plus Annual Censuses of Production;Dunne and Hughes (1990).

market proved more crucial. Thus, the dispersion of share ownership among financial institutions pursuing short-term strategies of
portfolio investment, the weakness of legal constraints on hostile
takeovers, and the possibility of purchasing assets with unsecured
company paper all combined to make acquisitions an attractive
alternative to internal growth for many British firms when share
prices soared (Hannah, 1983: chs. 7, 9; Williams *et al.*, 1983:
76–91; Cosh *et al.*, 1989; Fairburn and Kay, 1989). In the absence
of alternative sources of long-term finance such as a regional banking system (which gradually disappeared as a result of amalgama-
tions, concentration, and the construction of a national branch
network during the late nineteenth and early twentieth centuries),[3]
the persistence of these conditions has had a particular impact on
medium-sized enterprises whose numbers have continued to
decline through the 1980s unlike those of their smaller counterparts (Dunne and Hughes, 1990: 22, 94).

As once independent small and medium-sized firms were transformed into subsidiaries of larger national groups, links between
local enterprises waned and industrial districts lost their coherence. Many such firms were promptly closed down by their new
owners, while the surviving units were incorporated into the
centralised strategies and financial disciplines of multi-plant or
multi-divisional companies (Channon, 1973; Hill and Pickering,
1986; Goold and Campbell, 1987; Blackburn, 1982). Under these
conditions, local economies were transformed from integrated
productive systems into travel-to-work areas (Lovering, 1988), and
collaboration among economic actors was displaced upwards to
the national level. Business associations shed much of their local
focus, often through a deliberate process of regional amalgamation
and consolidation, while the largest firms increasingly abandoned
collective action altogether in favour of bilateral deals with trade
unions and government (Brown, 1980; Brown and Walsh, 1991;
Grant with Sargent, 1987).

Like the concentration process itself, this postwar trend towards
the disintegration of local economies was reinforced by the
intended and unintended consequences of government policies.
Thus postwar regional policies played an important part in this
process by pushing companies through financial incentives and
planning restrictions to situate new plants in development areas
far from existing industrial agglomerations (Wray, 1957: 55–67;
McCrone, 1969). So too did the reorganisation of local government in the 1960s into larger and more remote regional authori-

ties and the progressive restriction of its financial and political autonomy since the mid-1970s (Travers, 1989). At the same time, moreover, the growing salience of national government in a wide range of spheres from macroeconomic and industrial policy to education and social welfare led businessmen, trade unionists and other economic actors to look increasingly towards the centre rather than the locality for the solutions to their problems.

The resurgence of small firms?

To explain the decline of industrial districts in postwar Britain does not in itself account for why they have not re-emerged during the past two decades. A significant reversal of the historical trend towards increasing concentration in British manufacturing has taken place since the late 1960s. Thus the number of manufacturing firms with fewer than 100 employees has more than doubled since 1968 (though significant changes in census definitions and coverage have also been introduced during this period), while their share of output and employment have risen from 11.5 per cent and 13.5 per cent respectively to 19.3 per cent and 24 per cent in 1986. The share of firms with more than 1,000 employees, by contrast, declined from 69.8 per cent to 59.1 per cent of output and from 62.7 per cent to 52.8 per cent of employment during the same period.

Yet this quantitative resurgence of small firms in British manufacturing should not be taken as an unequivocal sign of qualitative revitalisation. First, the improvement in small firms' share of output and employment is almost entirely due to the disproportionate decline in that of larger firms during a period of dramatic contraction in British manufacturing. Second, mortality rates among small firms remain extremely high (almost half of new firms fail within five years, and nearly three-quarters within eleven years), while employment growth is heavily concentrated in a small number of rapidly expanding companies (less than 2 per cent of new businesses account for 25–50 per cent of jobs created in the medium term). Third, there has been no improvement in productivity or profitability of small firms relative to that of their larger counterparts since the 1970s (Storey and Johnson, 1987; Dunne and Hughes, 1990).

Behind this disappointing performance lies the fact that, despite their numerical expansion, British small firms remain relatively isolated from one another and rarely form part of dynamic inter-firm networks, whether geographically localised or not. This generalisation appears valid both for declining and for expanding sectors and regions. Thus, for example, a detailed study of the hosiery and knitwear industry in Leicester found that despite high levels of new firm formation (mainly by Asian immigrant entrepreneurs), there was little specialisation by process. Many companies consciously avoided subcontracting relationships, and those who engaged in them did so mainly to meet temporary peaks in demand (Cento Bull *et al.*, 1991). Similarly, a close examination of small high-tech firms in Cambridge likewise found that there were few links between local enterprises – whether commercial or technological – even where they were located beside one another in the same science park (Saxenian, 1989).

Even more significant, perhaps, is the relative absence or weakness of collaborative subcontracting networks between large and small firms in the UK. Thus despite growing volatility of demand, enhanced fashion sensitivity and increased flexibility requirements, large retailers in sectors such as clothing, textiles, furniture, and footwear rarely seem to have developed new collaborative relationships with more autonomous suppliers able to come up with saleable designs and adjust rapidly to changing market trends. Most retailers have instead taken advantage of high levels of competition to squeeze domestic manufacturers' profit margins, while remaining unwilling to offer prices adequate to support suppliers' investments in design capability and re-equipment for 'quick response' (Rubery *et al.*, 1987; Rubery and Wilkinson, 1989; Zeitlin and Totterdill, 1989; Walsh, 1991; Whitaker, 1991; Crewe and Davenport, 1992). In automobiles and electronics, similarly, despite manufacturers' ostensible commitment to new 'partnerships' with 'preferred' suppliers able to meet increasingly stringent demands for quality, innovation and just-in-time delivery, price remains central in contract allocation and inventory costs are often merely pushed on to subcontractors rather than reduced through cooperative efforts (Amin and Smith, 1991; Turnbull, 1991; Sako, 1992).

Why has the quantitative resurgence of small firms not given rise to a re-emergence of dynamic inter-firm networks, whether among small firms themselves or between firms of different sizes? One possible answer, suggested by the preceding discussion of subcontracting relationships, would emphasise the constraints imposed on small firms by pre-existing levels of economic concentration in the UK and the disproportionate power of large firms which flows from them. British manufacturing, as we have seen, was the most concentrated of all the advanced capitalist economies by the 1970s, and the share of large firms in output and employment despite its recent decline remains extremely high by international standards. Nor is this distinctiveness confined to production: retail distribution of most consumer goods is, if anything, more concentrated still. Thus by the late 1970s, for example, large retailers controlled more than 70 per cent of all clothing sales in the UK, compared to some 15 per cent in France and Italy, and despite some concentration in the latter countries during the 1980s, the contrast with the UK remains dramatic (Zeitlin and Totterdill, 1989: 157–8). Such high levels of concentration in industrial structure and retail distribution, it is widely believed, inhibits the development of autonomous small firms and collaborative supplier networks by restricting access to final markets and encouraging large firms to squeeze their dependent subcontractors. When greater capacities for product innovation and productive flexibility are required than those remaining among domestic subcontractors, retail chains and multinational manufacturers may then turn to more autonomous suppliers in other European countries such as Italy and Germany or even the Far East (Zeitlin and Totterdill, 1989: 167–70, 177; Crewe and Davenport 1992: 195).

We could also add to this analysis the effects of concentration in financial markets. Retail banking in the UK is concentrated in the hands of four large and two smaller national clearing banks, which avoid long-term industrial investments and lack a real regional dimension (Williams *et al.*, 1983: 58–76; Collins, 1988: ch. 12). Even when these national clearing banks are prepared to make loans to small firms, as they were on a considerable scale during the 1980s, they lack the local knowledge and sectoral expertise needed to assess with any reliability the prospects of success, and losses on such loans during the recession of 1988–92 were exceeded only by those on real estate (which often served as the collateral for the former) (Hall, 1989: 43–5; Gapper, 1993). Under these conditions, as noted earlier, growing firms seeking long-term finance are forced into a stock market dominated by large institutional investors that encourages further concentration through mergers and takeovers, which ran at higher levels in the 1980s than in any previous period (Cosh *et al*, 1989; Hughes, 1989).

There is clearly a good deal to this line of argument, and the inhibitory impact of large retailers, manufacturers, banks and the stock market figure prominently in most well-informed discussions of the obstacles to small-firm development in contemporary

Britain. Yet it doubtful whether these forces in themselves can provide a satisfactory explanation. For one thing, to explain the limited development of small firms by the power of the large is to redefine rather than to resolve the problem. For another, such an explanation is difficult to reconcile both with the manifest difficulties and decline of large manufacturers in the UK, and with the emergence of industrial districts and collaborative supplier networks in other advanced countries historically characterised by high if not fully comparable levels of economic concentration.

A second line of explanation, often put forward as a contrast with the Italian experience, focuses on socio-cultural obstacles in Britain to autonomous entrepreneurship and cooperation among economic actors. Thus, in Mauro Magatti's stimulating comparative study of Lancashire and Ticino Olona during the postwar period, a significant element in explaining the contrasting fortunes of the two textile districts is the absence of aspirations to and collective support for independent entrepreneurship among British workers. Lancashire textile workers, in Magatti's neo-Polanyian analysis, looked to trade union solidarity and the redistributive promises of the welfare state rather than to self-employment and reciprocity within kin and friendship networks as a solution to the problems caused by the decline of large textile companies (Magatti, 1991).

Here again, there is undoubtedly something to this argument. By the early nineteenth century, wage labour was much more widespread and self-employment accounted for a smaller proportion of the working population in the UK than in other European countries, not only in industry but also in commerce and agriculture, and significant differences have persisted in a number of cases even as the latter have reached comparable levels of economic development (O'Brien and Keydar, 1978: 70–1; Crossick and Haupt, 1984; Storey and Johnson, 1987: 34–7). Yet even in the UK, as the Oxford social mobility studies show, there are significant numbers of families with inter-generational traditions of self-employment (Goldthorpe, 1980: 258), while as we have seen, the rate of self-employment and new firm formation has increased sharply in recent years. Nor is there any necessary contradiction between trade unionism and collective defence of employment on the one hand and reciprocal support for individual entrepreneurship on the other, as the history of the 'Third Italy' itself amply demonstrates (Brusco, 1982; Sabel, 1982: 220–31; Trigilia, 1990).

At a deeper level, too, there is widespread evidence of reciprocity, trust and cooperation among local economic actors in contemporary Britain involving not only immigrant communities, as Magatti suggests (Magatti, 1991: 228–34, 340), but also native-owned businesses. In the 'silk triangle', for example, on the southern fringe of the former Lancashire cotton district, local firms lend one another scarce skilled workers and specialised machines, pass on orders to one another, and exchange information on new technology and market prospects (Pyke, 1987b, 1988). Similar practices of informal cooperation have likewise been reported among clothing, textile and engineering firms in other British districts such as Rochdale and Leicester (Cento Bull et al., 1991: 92–3; Penn, 1992: 220–1). As in the case of self-employment and new firm formation, the British problem appears less that of cultural barriers to the emergence of cooperation among economic actors than that of an unfavourable environment for its sustained development and diffusion.

A key element of this environment is the relative weakness or absence in the UK of local and sectoral associations of firms providing collective services to their members and concerting their policies in areas such as training, marketing, technology, R&D, finance, and industrial relations. For one of the most robust findings of international research is that, as a widely quoted adage puts it, the central problem facing small firms is not that of being small but that of being lonely (Pyke and Sengenberger, 1992: 11). Some comparative studies accordingly argue that the lack of collective organisation among small firms in the UK stems from the absence of a distinct artisanal sector, founded on a separate legal status and embodied in autonomous representative institutions, which could serve as the basis for collective identity and political influence (Jones and Saren, 1990). In this case, too, there can be little doubt that such contrasts highlight a significant feature of the British situation, while artisan associations and the legal definition of artisanal status have made an important contribution to small-firm development in countries such as Italy and Germany (Berger, 1980; Weiss, 1988; Lane, 1992: 79–81; Streeck, 1992). But here again, the proposed explanation remains seriously incomplete. For the legal and political definition of the artisanate as a distinct category may not be sufficient to prevent its economic decomposition, as the French case demonstrates (Zdatny, 1990). Conversely, too, the absence of such an institutional status need not form an insuperable obstacle to the establishment of vibrant collective associations in which small and medium-size firms actively participate. Thus in the UK, as we have seen, local trade and employers' associations were vital to the functioning of prewar industrial districts, and their decline is a relatively recent phenomenon. Elements of such collective organisation still survive among employers in many regions, while in some sectors such as footwear, industrial research associations have been increasingly active over the past decade in adapting computerised management and design systems to the requirements of smaller companies (Rubery and Wilkinson, 1989: 126, 129).

In most cases, however, the continued decline of business interest associations and collective service provision forms part of the broader disappearance in the UK of what Paul Hirst and I have called an 'industrial public sphere' (Hirst and Zeitlin, 1989b), a process for which the national state bears a heavy responsibility. Government policies, as we have seen, played a decisive role in the transformation of industrial structure and the disintegration of regional economies during the postwar period, though the outcomes did not always correspond precisely to the expectations of their architects. The 1945–51 Labour governments unsuccessfully sought to modernise fragmented industries by promoting tripartite collaboration with employers and unions and the provision of collective services through statutory development councils (Henderson, 1952; Mercer, 1991; Dupree, 1992). Since then British governments of all political stripes have defined their industrial policy options in terms of the appropriate balance to be struck between large, hierarchical firms on the one hand and free, self-regulating markets on the other. The cumulative effect of this vision – extending well beyond industrial policy to issues such as regional development, R&D, training and industrial relations – has been to sap the vitality of intermediary associations and inter-firm linkages, thereby leading the economy itself to approximate more closely to the institutionally impoverished environment presupposed by the policy-makers themselves.

Seen in this light, the policies followed by Conservative governments since 1979, with their distinctive combination of deregulation, privatisation and administrative centralisation, are merely the latest turn of the screw in a longer historical process which has undercut the conditions needed for the flourishing of industrial districts in the United Kingdom. Nowhere is this continuity more evident, paradoxically, than in the new policies aimed at promoting small business growth during the 1980s. Such policies addressed a wide range of problems from financial support for self-employment, new firm formation and capital investment through exemption from labour law and other regulatory 'burdens' to assistance with premises, technology transfer and export market. The common element of these policies – which largely accounts for their qualitative failure – is that they were aimed at encouraging the growth of individual small firms as representatives of a generic category rather than upgrading the performance of local or sectoral networks of small firms. Ironically, too, the main alternative to official policy – which has been gaining ground in recent years – is that public resources should be targeted on those smaller firms with the greatest potential for output and employment growth – assuming of course that such 'winners' can be credibly identified in advance (Storey and Johnson, 1987: ch. 7).

My reading of the comparative evidence as well as the UK's own historical experience suggests instead that dynamic small-firm development and the regeneration of local economies can best be promoted through the recreation of an 'industrial public sphere' within which a variety of relevant economic actors can collaborate in solving common problems. Flourishing industrial districts require a complex and variable ensemble of regulatory institutions for the provision of common services and the resolution of internal conflicts, together with strong local interest organisations capable of internalising the costs and benefits of such collective goods (Trigilia, 1991; Zeitlin, 1992). Informal cooperative practices and collective organisation among local economic actors have never completely disappeared, even in post-Thatcherite Britain, and public authorities can consciously stimulate the development of such districts by simultaneously fostering the creation of the institutional infrastructure and the collective actors required for their sustained reproduction. But such an approach obliges governments to renounce the imposition of industrial policies from above – whether based on strategic planning on the left or free-market deregulation on the right – in favour of a more demanding and uncertain process of social and political leadership in which establishing a dialogue and building a consensus among local interests becomes inseparable from analysing the weaknesses of the regional economy and constructing effective institutional solutions (Hirst and Zeitlin, 1991; Sabel, 1992).

A final but indispensable requirement for such a strategy concerns the autonomy of local government. Only local authorities, as comparative studies of successful districts show, are in a position to acquire the detailed knowledge of the local economy and broker the social consensus among local actors needed for the effective provision of collective services and the creation of an 'industrial public sphere'. Where political decentralisation has enhanced the autonomy and powers of regional government, as in Italy during the 1970s or Spain (and to a lesser extent France) during the 1980s, the reorientation of local interests and objectives may give a crucial boost to the development of industrial districts (Trigilia, 1992; Benton, 1992; Ganne, Chapter 7, this volume). Where the financial and political independence of local authorities are sapped by central government controls, as in contemporary Britain, industrial districts cannot flourish and promising experiments in collective service provision may wither on the vine (Hirst and Zeitlin, 1989a, b). It is on this dimension that British 'exceptionalism' among the other advanced economies has arguably been most pronounced over the past two decades (Crouch and Marquand, 1989). Hence it is difficult to imagine a sustained resurgence of small firms and local economies in the future without some devolution of central power to new regional authorities, a possibility which developments both inside and outside the United Kingdom – from Scotland to the European Union – fortunately keep returning to the political agenda.

Notes

1. Even here, however, analogous links between autonomous agrarian structure and diffused industrialisation can be identified for cases like Sheffield, Birmingham and West Yorkshire (see Sabel and Zeitlin, 1982).
2. For a survey documenting the continuing importance of regionally specialised industrial complexes in British manufacturing during the 1950s, see Burn (1958), especially the chapters on shipbuilding, cotton and rayon textiles, woollens and worsteds, pottery, and cutlery.
3. 'Until the 1880s English country banks were products of the localities and regions that they served; customers and shareholders were frequently the same people. The banks' constituencies both owned the banks and did business with them. Directors and managers knew their customers well and with prudence and local knowledge were prepared to go beyond the bounds of short-term lending' (Cottrell, 1992: 53). Between 1870 and 1920, however, there were 264 banking

mergers, 370 banks disappeared, and the share of deposits held by the five largest banks rose from 25 per cent to 80 per cent in England and Wales and from 20 per cent to 66 per cent in the UK as a whole. On the amalgamation movement and the decline of regional banking in the UK, see also Capie and Rodrik-Bali (1982); Collins (1991: 22–42). Up through the 1960s, smaller British firms could still raise capital through provincial stock exchanges which often specialised in particular industries (e.g. cotton in Manchester, iron and steel in Sheffield, motor vehicles in Birmingham), but their importance fell off sharply after 1945 (Thomas, 1973).

FRANCE: BEHIND SMALL AND MEDIUM-SIZE ENTER-PRISES LIES THE STATE

BERNARD GANNE

The destiny of small and medium-size enterprises in French socio-economic imagery has been a strange one. They have been variously reviled and adulated. In the aftermath World War II they symbolised the archaic state of French industry, only to become quite unexpectedly a model for countering the recession and an advanced prototype for new forms of flexible production. Thus they have successively had contradictory expectations put upon them which they cannot altogether fulfil. How then is one to choose and whom should one believe with, on the one hand, the view prevailing in the 1960s that 'industrial mergers should be speeded up' and 'marginal productive units' curbed, as advocated both by the employers' federation (CNPF) and INSEE,[1] and, on the other, the exhortations of economists in the 1980s who saw SME as the cutting-edge of the economy by which to counteract the 'crippling pervasiveness' of large industrial groups and the 'omnipresent state?'[2]

Yet behind and beyond the contrary cases put for large or small enterprises it is not difficult to detect an abiding feature of French practice: whatever view is propounded the higher administration and the government make it their business to be directly involved in the economy and shape the type of enterprise to be developed. Hence any mention made in France of the particularities of small and medium-size enterprises (SME) cannot fail to relate back to the larger political context from which they are inseparable and whereby they will be regulated. The specific nature of the French system is discernible less in the SME themselves than in the projection they are given by the state at various times. It is precisely this economic policy in regard to SME that we aim to outline here.

Evident though it may be, in the French context, that the discourse engaged in for or against the SME should not be seen for more than it is – (i.e. a position where each new conception sets out to correct the one pertaining before), it is nonetheless true that to include SME in a highly centralised politico-economic system is to accept the effect this has on their form of organisation and style of operation. Unquestionably this very presence of the state, discernible even at the level of production, comprises one of the special characteristics of the French system and marks it out unmistakeably as representing a mixed economy.

At all events this is the principal point of difference with Italy, where examples of 'spontaneous' or 'endogenous' development seemingly occurring without conscious interventionism on the part of the state, and has been the envy of more than one French technocrat. Without wanting to make too much of this, it is has to be recognised that the development and spread of SME-based autonomous industrial districts in central Italy is very probably not unconnected with the fact that the low visibility of central government is an enabling as well as a decisive factor. Production in the context of a centralised or non-centralised system gives rise to different constraints and different modes of organisation; this has perhaps in recent times been forgotten in part because of a too narrow focusing on the firm itself.

Without being direct – in the sense which at one stage the structuralist approach with its concern to display the state's determining role might have allowed it to be – the connection between economics and politics is all the closer in the French context in that in each case it appears to imply the way a whole system functions. To every type of 'governance' (Benko and Lipietz, 1992), so to speak, there seems to correspond an organisational phase of local economic systems that gives rise to forms of development specific to SME. Indeed, if one tries to establish a pattern of the place and significance of SME in the French productive system over a sixty-year period, there appear to be four distinct phases that correspond to as many political and economic phases or types of 'governance':

The state as mediator and the social model of family enterprises in the interwar period

The French productive system at that time appears – in relation, in particular, to Germany and Britain – to have been characterised by the large place accorded to family-run SME and localised industrial systems comprising small enterprises. But contrary to more recent image-making that tends to consider small structures as privileged units of resistance to a centralised hierarchy, their highly visible presence in the productive system was in fact a function of their place in the scheme of things then deployed by the state in its role as mediator, favouring a fragmented power structure at the local level, but one that was vertically integrated in a highly centralised fashion.

State emphasis on planning and consequent fall from favour experienced by SME in the post-war period

The whole system was called into question in the aftermath of the war and during the 1960s, at a juncture when the state as intermediary gave place to the state as prime mover in economic reconstruction, instigating and planning for industrial concentration. As a consequence the SME, in their customary fields especially, faced a marked decline at the very time when in Italy there was a proliferation of industrial districts that was later to arouse considerable envy.

Reinstatement of SME through a policy of cooordinated action

The force of the recession hit the state hard in its planning role, obliging it initially to take on what has been described as a 'stretcher-bearing' function (Cohen, 1989), coming to the aid of groups and playing down the emphasis on incentive in favour of greater dialogue at a local level. Restored to favour by virtue of their proven resilience, the SME thus became an important element in the policy embarked upon of coordinated consultation with local government.

Decentralisation and mobilisation around SME

Decentralisation accentuated recourse to SME so as to ensure active economic mobilisation on the part of local interests and authorities. But one of the effects of this development was paradoxically to enable the SME during the 1980s to expand beyond the locality. Be that as it may, the evidence in the case of France is that state interventionism and SME development are closely interlinked. Let us try to look more deeply at the thought governing each of these phases.

The interwar period: family-run SME, state as mediator and system of *notables*

With the high profile industrial concentration observed in the 1960 to 1980 period, one is inclined to overlook the fact that an abiding feature of France in the interwar years was the prevalence of SME and SME systems to a degree more pronounced than in Germany or Britain. Further, as a mode of organisation and a role model they received general validity whereby to fend off the spectre of the depression, overproduction and unemployment. SME, economic Malthusianism, cartels and combines seemed to constitute a system which, with the backing of the state as mediator, set out to establish itself as the one viable, responsible model for development through which to exorcise the distortions of unbridled capitalism and competition.

Hence both in theory and action, SME were promoted by a whole system of practice, not, as might be thought today, in opposition to the institutions of government but with their support.

An industrial structure bearing the imprint of SME

Economists and historians have remarked on the degree to which development after the 1920s was based essentially on devolution and a web of SME networks. Remaining highly 'individualistic, employers, who were wedded to a family-based entrepreneurial system and regional or segmented markets, with no concern to reach beyond', they deliberately developed a system of limited association in preference to combines (Bonin, 1988), and were mistrustful of financial markets with their profiteering and speculation, the chosen ground of confidence tricksters, as Alfred Sauvy reports (1984). (Sauvy's authoritativeness for this whole period hardly needs stressing.) In fact, reconstruction after 1919 had been carried out very rapidly; however, as one historian notes, 'too many firms' had perhaps 'rebuilt their factories precisely in the same way, without attempting to modernise and in particular without effecting concentration', with the result that 'what was new was no longer in fashion' (Bonin, 1988).

At all events in 1931, apart from some concentration in a few sectors and some instances of vertical integration, French industry showed little evidence of concentration in relation to that of its neighbours. The largest market capitalisations at the time – Saint-Gobain and Alsthom – represented no more than a fifteenth part of ICI or IG Farben. The electrical industry, where grouping might have been expected to be more self-evident than in other sectors, remained scattered among a large number of firms. Overall no fewer than two-thirds of all wage-earners belonged to firms with fewer than 100 employees and 40 per cent to firms employing fewer than 10 (Kuisel, 1984).

A Malthusian ideology that favoured SME

It has to be understood that this state of affairs was not simply the result of indifference or non-interference but of a deliberate policy. The period was one marked by an obsessive fear of over-production, the remedy sought being first to contain production and then to temper competition and favour agreements to produce less, thereafter calling on the government to adjudicate where necessary.

In the development of what Alfred Sauvy calls the spread of authentic 'economic Malthusianism' centred on the 'pursuit of rarity' (Sauvy, 1984) SME appear as a privileged instrument of support. Limiting production, organising agreements (in the inter-war period there were somewhere between 1,000 and 3,000 agreements within sectors to fix price scales and production quotas) and so weakening the rationale for concentration both for 'technical' reasons (the fight against overproduction) and ideological ones too (Sauvy quotes articles which show pride and satisfaction in France's 'timid yet flourishing economy as compared with the presumptuous and decadent economy of the Anglo-Saxon races'), such concerns could only work in favour of SME and reinforce their hold. Indeed, over the period a number of sectors and professions set themselves up as genuinely closed systems with government support.

The state as mediator, SME and system of notables, *or perpetuating the arrangement*

Certainly it is against this background that the continuing predominance of the SME and SME systems in the interwar period is best understood. The effect was intensified by a form of organisation in France that, where the economic sectors and, in the political context, central government were concerned, favoured an institutional system of vertical relations, itself determining a highly characteristic form of operation at a local level, known as the 'system of *notables*'.

In its activity, every SME and industry counted on its sector and its sector's negotiating with government to guarantee it a market and a continuation of its special position, as illustrated by the policy with regard to agreements and cartels. This vertical fragmentation was further boosted politically by the system of *notables*, the function of the *notable* being to guarantee and bolster internally a degree of diversity which he was entrusted with 'covering' *vis-à-vis* central government and the outside world. Therein lay both the *notable*'s strength and weakness, his power embodying at once his standing surety for the status quo, but as its hostage (Worms, 1966; Ganne, 1985).

In the interface it represents between the community and society at large the *notable*'s power thus depended directly on the centralised nature of the state. He was both a 'product of centralisation', thereby being allotted a special role, and answerable for it, with the result that the system was self-enclosed. In this respect one is a long way from the idea of 'autonomous power within a locality' as suggested by the Italian districts or even the American 'communities'. Giving expression to an 'ideal of decentralisation' which can be no more than imperfectly realised, 'communities' represent in some way the 'antithesis of the state'; whereas in France, across the system of *notables* in particular, the state remains essentially the 'frame of reference of actors in the locality' (Grémion, 1976).

Thus it is not in spite of, or for want of, the state that SME and diverse local industrial systems survived in prewar France but in close association with the state and, so to speak, with its blessing; and the system of *notables* as a form of local organisation was in perfect accord with this overall mode of functioning. Hence the fact of centralisation, far from suppressing local power, gave rise to it in specific forms (Grémion, 1976). In fact, contrary to what is thought to be the case with Italian districts, the important point is not the autonomy of the areas in question and their independence of organisation in relation to the higher authorities; rather their very links with the world of politics provide those at a local level with a defining role and a form of organisation, each side reinforcing the other; those at a local level counting on the state to guarantee the status quo, the Malthusian state in return finding in the continuance of fragmented local systems a guarantee of the qualified development it seeks. The circle is thus complete and the system contained within itself.

So it appears that the Malthusian policy prevailing between the wars and the interaction thus established with central government enabled the SME and local industrial schemes to hold their own and survive as a closed system – a system which was to be called into question *en bloc* once the war was over.

SME and the post-war modernising state

The aftermath of the war saw a start to the restructuring of industry that would lead to the disappearance of a whole string of smaller enterprises which at the time counted for a major part of the industrial fabric. Traditional sectors of industry producing consumer goods such as clothing, textiles, leather and so on underwent thorough reorganisation involving many closures. Considered apart from major industries affected by such restructuring, the SME legacy in terms of structure and variety that subsisted from the prewar period was a huge one. It covered textile centres in the Vosges, paper and leather systems in Annonay in the Ardéche, cutlery in Thiers, shoemaking in Fougères or Romans, small-scale metallurgy and the watchmaking industry in Franche-Comté as well as the Lyon silk systems with their ramifications in the surrounding countryside, in all a highly diffuse system of industrialisation based on smaller enterprises, which has still not been properly accounted for (Ganne, 1990) and which continued to play a vital role after the war. But the times had changed and the system of *notables* which had previously contributed to the SME's self-enclosed pattern was somewhat disrupted.

Indeed it was against the perpetuation of this rigid pattern, which appeared to give precedence to defending outdated local modes of organisation in the face of necessary change and adaptation, that the current in favour of planning and modernisation (Bonin, 1988) made its impact after the war, according the state a prime role in the task of reconstruction and then of coordinating economic concentration. Bearing in mind the then dispersed nature of industrialisation, the 1950s and 1960s witnessed the disappearance on a fairly massive scale of structures providing an 'alternative to mass production', as they have been called (Sabel and Zeitlin, 1985), with an attempt to make decentralisation fill the gap.

Modernisation by concentration – destruction of former systems of activity

With a view to effecting the necessary modernisation of the productive apparatus, the series of Plans – focusing as they did particularly on capital goods industries, and principally on larger enterprises in order to realise coherent entities – orchestrated the restructuring of industry during the 1960s and 1970s. In their different ways the 'ardent obligation of the Plan' extolled in the 1960s and the 'industrial imperative' of the 1970s encapsulated the centralised economic process *à la française* which, by aiming to give 'coherence' and 'uniformity' to industrial structures, necessarily proscribed the multiplicity and diverseness of localised industrial systems.

The policy of national and regional development (*aménagement du territoire*) had as its initial purpose to bring about a more rational distribution of industrial activity, but gradually in the endphase of Gaullism and under Georges Pompidou it became a spearhead for economic policy, organising industrial mergers, setting up coastal industrial complexes with port facilities, and practising an active interventionism which met with the full approval of social actors on the right as well as on the left. The SME and old localised industrial systems represented so many pockets of backwardness that called for restructuring under the modernisation programme. The programme, which had the full support of government and was on occasion imposed on the economic actors, received substantial implementation wherever traditional industries proliferated. So it was that many smaller enterprises disappeared with in fact little resistance being shown, in spite of a few token conflicts that provided evidence enough of the highly 'segmented' character of the localised systems described above and the price it was necessary to pay.

Persistence and emergence of a few localised industrial systems

However, in spite of the vast number of closures, the same period saw a few cases of SME and SME systems developing in some French regions, cases that in their pattern of emergence were not unlike those observed in the so-called Third Italy. Such cases were especially noticeable in Brittany, Anjou and in the region of Cholet (Vendée) in the west; and in the Jura, Savoy and the Monts du Lyonnais in the east.

What these regions had in common was their relative independence or rather isolation in cultural, social, political as much as economic terms, thereby calling to mind remarks made by Bagnasco and Trigilia in relation to the 'white' (Catholic) area round Bassano and the red zone of the Valdelsa (Bagnasco, Trigilia, 1988). In any case, it is clear that dispersed industrialisation and SME with their self-enclosed systems developed in areas that are ideologically distinctive[3] and with an urban system where the principal market town has a decisive role. Minguet, whose studies of the Cholet region are well known, observes that so as not to break down this system, in fact to reinforce it, industrial units were often spread across a number of villages rather than concentrated in one place (Minguet, 1983).

At all events, such instances remained restricted and exceptional during a phase of industrial concentration and restructuring in which the state was the driving force for modernisation, prioritising the organisation of coherent industrial groups producing capital goods (Laborie, Langumier and De Roo, 1985) and considering that SME had no more than a 'marginal' role[4] to play (i.e. calling into question the entire system as it had operated).

Full rein to state interventionism and retreat from system of 'notables'

Indeed the interventionist style of government with its mission to modernise brought to bear quite different methods that disrupted the previous system pertaining, the system that depended on the '*notables*'. The state as actor orchestrating first the reconstruction and then the modernisation of industry scaled up its efforts and administration to reach into every locality. Throughout this whole period increasingly well-manned echelons of central administration were transferred and set up within *départements* and the as yet unconstituted regions, so as to reach out ever more effectively at a local level where in a sense they duplicated representatives on their own ground.

The various ministries, including those of industry and equipment with which we are more directly concerned here, thus extended out regionally, the better to carry through national directives in regard to regional development and industrial policy. Development commissions (*missions d'aménagement*) directly responsible to the Prime Minister or, via the DATAR, to the Minister of Equipment were established within regions to prepare in detail such schemes as those involving setting up the eight metropolitan areas (across the OREAM, Organization d'études d'aires metropolitaines) or to oversee the carrying through of the major coastal industrial complexes and so on.

Local communities, though certainly brought in to consultation and decision-making but accorded little initiative, as was patent enough for instance in the implementation of urban development via the SDAU (Schémas Directeurs d'Aménagement Urbains) carried out through the department-based services of the Ministry of Equipment and its specialist economic section, were as often as not involved in a new style of relationship characterised by fairly high profile confrontation and direct supervision that cut right across the intermediate layers of what constituted the former system of '*notables*', thenceforth marginalised. Through the intermediary of these new channels, and with its mission to modernise the state imposed its will through its various intervention sectors – industry, equipment, health and so on – down to the level of every locality. However, the sudden incidence of the recession had a marked effect in restraining the impetus of the omnipresent state.

Recession and return of SME: from centralised state to coordinated consultation

With the recession biting and taking hold in the mid-1970s, a dual reappraisal took place. It signified on the one hand a boost for the

SME, whose resilience confounded earlier predictions, particularly in their ability to assimilate new technologies and confront new markets, while the state, whose initial impulse was to rescue the major lame-duck industries, quickly accepted the long-term impossibility of an obstructive stance in the face of necessary change. Its emphasis therefore shifted from regulation to active mobilisation, and from a somewhat imperative, centralised interventionism to embrace far wider concertation with the economic actors and local communities.

The SME's return to favour

After their earlier fall from grace and their subsequently restricted fortunes, SME provided unexpected evidence of their ability to withstand the recession. 'SME are better able to resist than the major enterprises' a key INSEE survey concluded (Amar, 1987). Between 1977 and 1984 they gave proof of standing up better than the larger enterprises by moving into markets within sectors hit by the recession. Employment levels and margins were better maintained. If exports fell and investment eventually showed signs of flagging, over the period their financial position and profitability were stronger.

Further, with the disarray that affected overall industrial production they appeared to be a source of strength in the changes taking place. The need for rapid adaptability to markets, for proven quality and – so as to achieve quality across new technologies – for flexibility in organisation and comeback, in a word, for reliability of product gave the SME a determining role in setting up a more resilient productive system. Thus SME sprang back into favour when least expected to, and the effect of the recession was to call into question the entire system of centralised state intervention previously installed with its regional ramifications.

From compulsory interventionism to concerted action

The response of the government was a dual one. With its fears for the economy and a virtual monopoly for intervention in the face of adversity it stood by to bale out major enterprises and safeguard major industrial sectors. At the same time, aware of reaching the limit of this course of action, it began to experiment and search for other forms of intervention that would promote greater activity and be more widely collaborative.

Initially, confronted by the drop in activity produced by the various oil shocks and fall in investment, government felt compelled to apply a more selective interventionism in favour of sectors seen to be potentially profitable or of greater strategic importance. The dual effect of this was to accelerate the concentration of state aid on the larger groups and in effect abandon other non-preferential sectors including SME (except when they were in dire straits), so accentuating the 'bipolarisation' of French industry. In 1976, for instance, seven major industrial groups – Thomson, CGE, CIT-HB, Alsthom-Atlantique, Empain, Dassault and SNIAS – collected 50 per cent of the total aid to industry, the equipment industries taken together counting for three-quarters (Laborie, Langumier and Roo, 1985).

However, without abandoning its interventionist style, the government had already begun, before the recession, to reach into spheres – in regional development, in particular – beyond its direct involvement. Its aim was to overcome the disadvantages of too diffuse, hence ineffective, initiatives. Responding to precise but unilaterally determined requirements, it was induced to build up a more horizontal system of organisation in the course of the 1970s in conjunction with local authorities; the effect of the recession was to accelerate this trend. Thus a programme for development that emanated from the top and was strongly 'recommended' gave way gradually to one that was based less on sectors, hence more comprehensive, and above all involved far greater consultation; one that resorted to devices of horizontality, negotiated in particular via agreements with medium-sized towns and rural districts. Thereby the ground was prepared for an eventual transfer of responsibility – including that of intervening in the economic field – to local authorities that took place under the terms of the Act of Decentralisation. Hence the system underwent a sharp reversal with specific local agreements and agreements between the government and the several regions supplanting the scatter effect of previous specific, sector-based initiatives.

The system of *notables*, a highly compartmentalised one as has been shown, working in conjunction with a form of state intervention that favoured highly specialised vertical relations of a functional type based on the various services of central administration, all this gave way to a system that sought, by way of agreements and a more horizontal style of management, to develop a wider form of concertation and one involving to a certain extent the opening up of local communities. In the course of the Giscard presidency profound changes took place in the politico-economic system, changes induced as much by the recession as by ancillary factors, since the state was unable on its own to resolve increasing misgivings about a policy of interventionism directed at ailing enterprises which was running ever more out of steam (Cohen, 1989). The problem seemed to emanate from the exclusive nature of state intervention in the economy, at which precisely the legislation on decentralisation carried through at the start of the 1980s was directed. Thus the policy of concertation served to pave the way for decentralisation.

The SME as activating agents: decentralisation and accompanying drawbacks

The arrival of the Left in power in the 1980s saw the economic mobilisation and development of local communities, its instrument being the legislation involving decentralisation and its chosen ground the SME.

The preliminary draft for the IX Plan sought to denounce the 'crippling gigantism' of the larger industrial groups, while recommending the SME as the 'leading edge of the economy' and the most effective 'bastion against monopolistic capitalism and the *all-encroaching* state'.[5]

Bearing in mind, however, the French context and the system previously prevailing. These initiatives in favour of better integration and a more direct role in development on the part of local actors inevitably led to some confusion, with the SME tending to develop their activities along professional and often non-local lines rather than strictly within localities. These various tendencies and the paradoxes of the current situation require a closer examination.

Decentralisation and ensuing problems

Contractual policies developed during the earlier phase had certainly brought the state closer to local communities; in particular, they had enabled a highly *dirigiste* and compartmentalised system of operation to be simplified, so becoming less rigid and more effective in its overall approach to problems, above all more attuned to the actors involved. Nevertheless the state continued to be the initiator. Having accepted the principle of partnership, it must concede responsibility.

The idea behind regionalisation was precisely to endow local authorities with genuine legal capability and thus allow them to be genuinely free to take action in a number of spheres that were hitherto the special province of the state, in particular where economic questions were concerned. Even if the transfer of power remained subject to control, with government maintaining its prerogatives and only envisaging autonomy in policy-making on the part of local communities – and of regions, in particular – insofar as it represented agreements actually entered into, the change is worthy of note. During the 1980s a number of regions formulated their own economic policies, to a large extent focusing on SME.

But it was above all in the sphere of support and subsidy that gradual changes made themselves felt. Observation shows how with such systems being set up at regional level, a model that prioritised larger enterprises in difficulty by way of direct financial aid enabling them to purchase capital goods gave way to another model, which was focused far more on aid to smaller industries and to the overall consolidation of the entire industrial fabric. In a move away from the previous philosophy, indirect support became much more the pattern, with initiatives undertaken for non-quantifiable investment in research, management, organisation, technology and so on.

One might have thought that such change would revitalise local development, but a different picture emerges. In some areas, where particular types of industry are located, Toulouse and the aeronautical industry, for instance, new SME cropped up to produce a degree of local integration, but they tended to form part of an ever-widening professionalised framework. Many studies of areas that were once industrialised or had thriving rural industries begin by pointing to the disappearance of 'horizontal solidarity' (de Banville, 1984). Recent research carried out in French *technopoles* has shown how tenuous are the links between groups of SME and the local environment, competitiveness counting for more than local loyalty or cooperation. In particular, a study of areas where industrialisation is scattered (one involving a comparison with Italy) stresses the significance of the restructuring taking place and the increasing effect of external networks (Ganne, *et al.*, 1988).

Hence, just when the time seems ripe for local integration, the model favoured by the new SME turns out to be one based on an association of professional ability which inevitably reaches beyond the locality. The pattern of industry is thus turning out to be less and less localized; in this sense the notion of 'territory' as a network is gradually taking the place of what has been described as 'territory as area' (Beckouche *et al.*, 1986). The 'reterritorialisation' of SME activities and systems appears to be going ahead more on the basis of an increased mobilisation of external resources than on that of locality. Does that imply that factors which should have favoured local integration in fact helped produce the opposite effect? The contradiction is more apparent than real.

Contradictions and further obstructions in the system

One of the consequences of the whole procedure of contractual development set up during the earlier phase through contracts involving medium-sized towns and rural areas appears to have been a degree of uniformity at local level. It was a time when a number of smaller towns and rural areas, where development had been slow, endeavoured to provide themselves with basic amenities (car parks, arts centres, whatever was needed) and undertake environmental improvements such as shopping streets, pedestrian precincts and so on; and, further, make premises available to self-employed craftsmen and owners of small industrial enterprises.

Contracts entered into led to a relative standardisation of all such provisions, involving certain norms of service and material. Whereas previously supervision of local authorities had proved essential so as to safeguard against hazards and uncertainties, the degree of uniformity established coupled with the fact that the areas, however diverse, tended in the end to adopt a similar model made for proportionately fewer differences, hence uncertainties. For this reason, local communities no longer represent an uncertainty requiring supervision nor initially a problem, and thus there is greater freedom to develop externalised systems. In this respect, contracts established with medium-sized towns and rural areas on the basis of concertation have currently enabled highly externalised systems to be deployed. This corresponds closely to the tendencies becoming apparent in new modes of production.

Inasmuch as the SME which resist are not, as in the past, subcontracting SME who are banking on the low cost of their workforce, but highly specialised SME making use of their technology and their flexibility, not in order to produce a greater quantity but to improve the quality of production of specific lines. What they regard as important is less the material aspect of their operation (workforce, premises, where basic services are now in most cases provided for locally) than being connected up with service and specialised professional systems, which are more often than not situated within a radius well beyond the locality.

The paradox is that all this has taken place just when the legislation on decentralisation appeared to favour a form of better integrated local or regional development. But it is also the case that the implementation of regionalisation has led to a number of problems that are only too typical of the French pattern. Though decentralisation has indeed conferred greater responsibility upon local communities, it has done so at the cost of making them more inter-competitive, a cost simply because of the fragmented nature of the French system.

After a long period of out-and-out centralism, tempered it is true by a moderate dose of concertation, it is scarcely surprising that the various communities want to exercise their new powers, including their economic powers, to the full. Each one within its limits set about developing the functions which it had until then seen carried out by the central authority; each one sought to equip and organise itself in order to become as nearly as possible an autonomous entity, endowed with whatever was needed to attract, if possible ahead of the others – so in the face of the others – this or that industrial firm and the by-products of growth. Without going so far as to become so many little self-sustaining republics (which they lack the means to be), there is at the present time a temptation for local communities to build up their amenities to the point of being able to offer as much as another, if not more; forgetting at the same time that current demand is concerned less with a full range of on-the-spot amenities as with whether or not the neighbourhood is a high-performance one that will offer effective opportunities to link in to networks and services the better to handle demand. Hence the problem is not so much one of amenities as of linking and communication, or, rather, the amenity at a premium is communicability, it being essential to be located in areas that are, so to speak, 'plugged in' to networks and capable of constituting pivotal points of communication; an imperative that is perhaps less onerous than having to sustain an investment programme that may turn out to be counter-productive.

Against such a background, too great an emphasis on locality in regard to the enterprise and its environment is likely to be way off the mark, even derisory, a source of satisfaction to no one but the elected representatives who thought up the scheme. In the French context where *communes* are excessively fragmented it is likely to court danger by setting each one against the other instead of inducing them get together and create viable entities and go for complementarity. Indeed, nowadays no single area can claim to respond to the new types of demand being made by enterprises. At the very least they call for a multiple area – the message is getting across – so as to enable an optimum response to be deployed through the activation of a number of networks, regional, subregional, extraregional too, rather in the way that has been observed in former districts in Italy.

So, because it unthinkingly reproduces a pattern of what is at once self-enclosed and a microcosm of republican centralism, a pattern for adoption at the level of *communes*, the 'localist' perspective focused as it is on mainly internal and integrated area development seems increasingly out of touch with specialisations that are currently observed and demands for access to the various networks and services, which for enterprises now represent the principal means of monitoring their environment, one that nowadays goes considerably beyond their immediate locality. In its self-integrating form, localism is perhaps out of line with the system of networks as it is now developing.

But just as enterprises which at one time thought of themselves as autonomous competing entities now, though still in competition, endeavour to play the game of cooperation and complementarity and become grouped in networks with the emphasis on specialisation and high performance, so one may hope that local communities may soon be drawn into more profitable dialogue and thus become better organised. Such a step needs to be taken if communities are to adapt to the emerging pattern of network development that now characterises the SME.

Summary

What conclusions can be drawn from this brief survey about the activity and development of SME and SME systems in the context of France? The success of the Italian districts with their small-scale enterprises, and perhaps regrets for having in the past – and especially in France – ignored the local dimension of industrial development and of SME have probably played their part in making something of a fetish of a model of local development that is highly 'endogenous', 'homogeneous', 'spontaneous', where the 'local' organisational forms of SME, often understood to be essentially 'cultural' would somehow interact with economic forces and thus mitigate their excesses. But surely this suggests itself as a response to a problem of the time, a scheme devised to mobilise as many local and institutional actors as possible the better to confront the recession; and at the same time stay in this recognisably French enclosure where paradoxically it is somehow the state that seeks thus to produce effects that are 'spontaneous and endogenous'

The French case would appear to present two points of interest: it displays unequivocally the structure of a mixed economy, and this is seemingly a fundamental feature of the French situation; more especially it displays a multiplicity of forms that afford so many means of interlinking economies and politics. Intervention on the part of the state is all too often seen only as direct intervention, whereas it seems more profitable to consider how the economic and political factors can interweave and be made to coalesce, and how it is by thus coalescing, by the 'involutions' thus occurring so to speak, that development can be mastered.

At all events, we have seen how the high visibility of SME in France during the interwar period was in no sense a marginal phenomenon but very much an integral part of a centralised political system that prevailed upon industry to adopt a position and an organisation *vis-à-vis* the state as mediator and regulator. Furthermore, the relatively closed and rigid character of the former industrial districts in France turns out to have been perfectly appropriate to the then mode of political organisation at a socio-territorial level with the system of *notables* as it has been described, both maintaining and perpetuating a highly compartmentalised functioning of local institutions.

It was indeed a specific politico-economic system and such was its development. When the state assumed the role of planner and moderniser it had the task of breaking these entrenched currents of influence and the impasse to which the system seemed to be leading, as was observed in the postwar period and the 1960s with central government spreading tentacles into local communities and displacing the system of *notables*. In this way, 'modernisation' imposed unilaterally with a view to realising economic concentration, was effected at the expense of SME.

The recession showed how fragile this Jacobin strategy was and demonstrated too the unexpected resilience of the SME and their advantage in adaptability. Recourse was then had to more comprehensive, better concerted methods by way of a policy that initiated agreements and contracts whereby local communities could be brought more directly into the development process. But, paradoxically, the degree of social and cultural conformity that resulted did not impede the outside development of SME and SME networks, as recently observed in the new system of flexible specialisation now underway. This has occurred in spite of legislation on decentralisation which has given a degree of autonomy to local and regional authorities, at the same time as has been suggested, a characteristically French paradox – resulting in a centralising republican pattern emerging here and there at a local level, so that the form of integration settled upon has often been an outdated one and inclined to aggravate competitiveness between local communities. These seem to be the issues at the present moment.

Thus it is that across SME and their varying role in the French politico-economic system, one can clearly discern the overall changes in the political process. In any event, SME and modes of governance prove here to be closely linked, and perhaps one can see better how essential it is, when seeking to have a proper understanding of the development of SME in France, to reposition them within the political and administrative strategy of intervention.

Notes

1. Declaration made by Ambroise Roux at the CNPE General assembly, quoted by Bucaille and Costa de Beauregard (1987: 15).
2. Preparatory report on the IX Plan 1984–1988 (Documentation Française, 1983).
3. In the case of the Vendée and the area round Cholet we are dealing with a 'whiter than white' region, that is ultra-Catholic and has a long royalist tradition. With the Jura and areas like Oyonnax it is the old utopian socialist, libertarian tradition that is to the fore.
4. Declaration by Ambroise Roux, see Note 1.
5. See Note 2

CONCLUSION: TURNING THE PAGE IN INDUSTRIAL DISTRICTS

CHARLES F. SABEL

A new curiosity

Every important debate begins with a surprising finding that flies in the face of settled understandings and ends with a second, related discovery that is, just as surprisingly, beyond the reach of the answers to the first. In the case of industrial districts the initial finding was that from the mid-1970s onwards agglomerations of small and medium-sized firms using a modern version of craft methods could compete successfully in a wide range of industries in world markets thought until then to be the preserve of large, vertically integrated corporations (see Pyke *et al.*, 1990). The finding that will, I believe, turn the page in the industrial district debate is that, as many of the preceding chapters have noted, competition between firms organised on Japanese principles of just-in-time or inventoryless production and the craft model of the industrial districts reveals unsuspected limits in the districts division of labour. Some of the very features connected to the acquisition and deployment of craft skill that allow the districts to respond more quickly to changing markets than the mass producers turn out to block the effective use of the wealth of information about the possibilities for improvement and innovation that operation under stringent inventoryless conditions brings to light. These limits, as several of the chapters also suggest, are not insuperable. But the result of the current competition between the district or craft model on the one hand and the Japanese system on the other, I believe, will be an amalgamation of the features of both that transforms the character of each. Relations within and among firms in the districts will be disciplined by an organised scrutiny of the division of labour that does not respect craft principles, and the closed, quasi-familial relations between employees and firms and among firms themselves in the Japanese system will come to have the fluidity now characteristic of the districts. If this is so, then the industrial districts will have a future, and it will not be one of simple assimilation to a superior model – but neither will it be an extrapolation of the development that brought them so conspicuously to attention in the first place. In this sense a discussion of the districts as they are and may well become must be as concerned with the self-limiting, unexamined assumptions of the industrial district debate as with its illuminating originality.

This conclusion begins, accordingly, by recalling just what was disconcerting in the discovery of the districts' success and reviewing, from a participant's point of view, the debates that resulted from the clash of differing explanations of that discovery. Then the focus shifts from differences among the explanations to a crucial feature they shared: a view of craft as a natural, historically evolving clustering of activities into trades or disciplines, and a way – or rather the way – to overcome the rigidities of hierarchy by combining theoretical and practical knowledge in apprenticeship so that mature craft workers can participate in conceptualising the tasks they execute.

The argument proceeds in three steps. First, I show how the understanding of craft as natural domains of activity and the acquisition of skill in apprenticeship leads to jurisdictional disputes and the creation of skill hierarchies which limit the very reintegration of conception and execution that is the cardinal virtue of this model of production. The reference is primarily to recent experience in large German firms, long regarded as pioneers in the organisation of modern craft systems; but analogous arguments help explain the difficulties of coordination currently observable among firms in the Italian or south-west German industrial districts. Next, I contrast the craft system with the Japanese production model in which the reintegration of conception and execution is institutionalised as a continuous commentary on the shortcomings of current operations and hence on the possibilities for redefining the division of labour among workers within a single work group, work groups within a firm, or among a firm and its suppliers. Because evaluation of current efforts is so closely connected with the exploration of new possibilities and the definition of joint goals I call this system learning by monitoring. The purpose is to show how such a system can overcome the limitations of Fordist hierarchy without producing obstructive internal divisions of its own. Finally, I turn the tables and speculate on the possibility that some of the institutional preconditions of the Japanese system as currently constituted may in fact limit the fullest deployment of learning by monitoring and how, suitably redirected, some of the institutions most closely associated with the industrial districts may provide a more hospitable setting for the application of the novel principles.

Whether I am right or wrong in the intuition that a recombination of features of the craft and Japanese systems will result in a distinctive form, I hope at least to be guided throughout the discussion by the same respect for the inventiveness of the economic actors and their constant capacity to extend the list of forms of association that turn out to be possible that, beyond all misleading differences and self-deceiving agreement, unites so many of those in the industrial districts and those fascinated by them.

Novel answers to classic questions

The debate about industrial districts commanded broad theoretical and practical attention because it raised fundamental questions about Adam Smith's claim that increases in efficiency depend on increases in the division of labour. This classic claim has dominated thinking about industrial organisation from the industrial revolution almost down to the present. It is the idea that a top-of-the-widget maker and a bottom-of-the-widget maker working together produce more widgets per unit time than two whole-widget makers. The argument is that the specialists have an easier time perfecting the skills needed for narrow tasks than the generalists and waste less time shifting from activity to activity than did the latter. Perhaps most important, the more specialised and simplified the task, the easier it is on this view to design a special purpose or dedicated machine to perform it more or less automatically, and hence the easier it is to mechanise production in general. Taken together these arguments make it plausible that under the right conditions there can be economies of scale, in which costs per unit of output decrease with an increase in total production (Smith, [1776] 1976).

Two general conclusions followed. The first was that increases in efficiency depend on the separation of conception from execution in production. Those who design products and the tasks and machines required to make them are distinct from those who execute the tasks and tend the machines: semi-skilled workers followed instructions, subcontractors followed blueprints. Hierarchy thus became the handmaiden of efficiency. The second conclusion was that the economy is (almost) self-contained, and in that sense distinct from the society that surrounds it. Because efficiency increased with the division of labour, firms got more productive as they dedicated a greater proportion of their resources to specialised purposes. So long as the organisational costs of extending the division of labour were small compared to the gains, the most efficient firm could cut its costs and hence increase its market share by further extensions. Each industry would thus in time come to be dominated by one or, at most, a few large firms; and because each of these stood to gain substantially from whatever was good for the industry as a whole, such good would in fact be provided out of self-interest by the dominant firms themselves. 'Society' would act almost invisibly in the background to provide the basic skills and rules of economic exchange required by all industries and not in the immediate interest of any to provide by itself. These were the principles that shaped the development and self-definition of mass production industry from the late nineteenth century through the 1970s (Chandler, 1977; Williamson, 1985).

The districts' successes directly challenged the Smithian logic of development and conclusions that followed from it (Piore and Sabel, 1984). Evidently, general-purpose, flexible machines combined with general skills could produce competitive products, where general skills means just the ability to apply general-purpose equipment to many purposes. Whether this result was only now possible because of the development of a novel class of general-purpose machines as typified by numerically controlled, programmable machine tools, or whether (as the historical record seemed to indicate) there were nineteenth- and twentieth-century precedents for and even linear ancestors of the current alternative systems, was less important than the challenge current developments posed to the Smithian understanding of the division of labour.

If the districts' success was not the transient result, say, of the large firms' temporary difficulties in adopting new technologies and organisational principles, or temporary growth in demand for just what the districts made, then the two consequences of the standard idea of the division of labour were untenable. First, the competitive combination of general-purpose equipment and general skills showed that the (re)integration of conception and execution must have efficiency advantages. The operator's or subcontractor's skill consists in determining how to perform the task assigned, and if, as is often the case, the task cannot be performed as described or could be performed more effectively if redefined, then helping to redefine it. The operators thus instruct themselves in executing the task, and instruct those responsible for its definition in their task as well. This amounts, of course, to the reintegration of conception and execution. The districts' experience suggests that such reintegration works: it reduces the costs of coordinating complex activities (if the operators make their own rules, no one needs to be paid to make rules for them); the experience of solving problems that arise in instructing oneself leads to the uncovering of possibilities for development missed – the operators see at first hand the consequences that instructions produce when told only to follow orders. The costs of hierarchy turned out to be greater than expected, the benefits smaller. Or to put the point in a related way, the districts showed that the greater the variety of production problems firms solved, the less it cost to solve further varieties and these economies of scope could rival economies of scale as a source of efficiency, thus reducing the cost differential between customised and standard items.

Second, there is nothing in the logic of this flexible, general-purpose system to suggest that its constituent production units, alone or in aggregate, will from immediate self-interest create a self-contained economy by providing all the services they need to operate. To see why, consider the (increasingly common) situation of a centralised mass producer trying to increase the flexibility of its operations by turning its operating units into the basal unit of the industrial districts: one or more general-purpose machines under the control of a corresponding number of skilled operators. Part of the operators' skill is knowing which services – heat treatment of a particular kind, new tooling, supplemental training, engineering consultation, and so on – are required for each task. Indeed, in a sense the operators' skilled autonomy consists precisely in the freedom to choose the services required and help define how they will be provided; absent that freedom, the operators simply execute the instructions of those who are authorised to serve the operation and the system remains as centralised as before. But if the operators do have this freedom, then all the services within giant, mass-production firms – everything from the research labs to the process engineering unit to the purchasing department – lose the stable markets on which they depend, and, unable to justify their existence by their sales performance, face closure. Yet nothing guarantees that firms on the outside market will perceive the incipient, fragmented demand for specialised services that does emerge from the flexible production units.

Here, of course, is where the social construction of the market comes in (Bagnasco, 1985). All the constituent production units appreciate in theory that they will be better off if there are institutions charged with providing the production-related – or, the Italians say, 'real' – services not available through the market, even if they all also know that none has a sufficient interest to create such an institution by itself. All also have some direct experience of the benefits of cooperating with other specialised producers as part of their everyday activities. Somehow, under favourable conditions, the general appreciation combines with the direct experience to produce cooperative creation of the web of service institutions that characterise districts. The process is no more obscure than the one by which a large group of persons endows itself with laws and a constitution (which also provides benefits to the aggregate of participants but not necessarily to any particular ones) – but it is no more transparent, either. Whatever its precise nature, this process supposes such a direct and reciprocal influence between the definition of society as a solidary community of fate and the construction of the institutions of economic solidarity that it is necessary to reverse the Smithian conclusion of the separation of society and economy as the price of progress and to speak instead of the efficiency advantages of reintegrating them. Thus, the Marshallian industrial district (see Becattini, 1987, 1990 for the connection to the work of the British economist Alfred Marshall) came to be understood as an agglomeration of independent, flexible units each able to achieve economies of scope because of its cooperation with the others.

Critical views of the industrial districts

These counter-conclusions elicited in turn three main kinds of response. Each corresponded to a classic current of social and political thought. Each illuminated important ambiguities in the original formulations. Each – inevitably? – was too self-absorbed to re-examine its own fundamental convictions in the light reflected back from its criticisms of the characterisation of the new situation. But neither did the proponents of the district view wind up learning much from their critics. In two cases, I think, it proved too easy to dismiss the criticisms as obtuse, or in any case as the reflex of prior concerns that did not have to involve students of the industrial district. In the third case the problem was the reverse: The criticism seemed more like an invitation to argue about the precise characterisation and evaluation of a phenomenon whose fundamental properties were well understood, rather than a challenge to the Marshallians' fundamental understanding. I examine the criticisms briefly in turn.

The Marxist criticism was the most critical, and for obvious reasons, Marxists believe that the development of the division of labour eventually results in the reintegration of conception and execution. Hence they held the first counter-conclusion for a theoretical possibility. But Marxists also believe that this can occur only when property has been socialised so that the producers, as owners of their products, will recognise their work in their works, and thus have the motive and opportunity to regard themselves as simultaneously conceiving and executing their tasks. Until then, the large firm in the Smithian sense counts as the motor of progress by increasing economic efficiency and heightening, through the collateral effects of the division of labour on the distribution of wealth, income, skills, and employment, the social pressures leading to the socialisation of property.

From this perspective the claims that new forms of cooperation emerging within a regime of private property allowed the reintegration of conception and execution looked like a naive or wilfully deceptive apology for new forms of exploitative control by the familiar large-firm actors (Amin and Robins, 1990; Harrison, 1994). Decentralisation of production to (non-union) outside subcontractors, for example, was seen as a way of escaping regulation of production through collective bargaining; internal decentralisation through the encouragement of cooperation between workers and managers was seen as a new technique for reducing the workers' collective control over their own situation.

There were, of course, manipulative uses of the new organisational techniques that left the *de facto* (to say nothing of the *de jure*) distribution of property rights as it had been; large firms transformed their internal organisation rather than simply decomposing into small units; and smaller firms grew, often establishing new operations in distant locations. The Marxists might have tried to advance debate and refine their own theory of economic transformations by distinguishing the operation and organisation of firms of all sizes that reinforced existing property and authority relations from productive decentralisation and cooperation that undermined them. Instead the Marxists used anything that might possibly count as a counter-example to the counter-examples to challenge the idea that anything new was afoot or even possible. As it became clear that the changes in progress, whatever their precise nature, were too sweeping and disruptive of established ways to be dismissed as a manipulative adjustment of old actors to new conditions, the search for sham looked more and more like the victory of the thirst for *Schadenfreude* over intellectual and political curiosity.

A second, contrary, and Hayekian response came from practitioners such as management consultants and business writers. The practitioners knew the large, US mass-production corporations. They could tell the difference between a manipulative fad and a dramatic change of course, although they had no qualms about extracting all the faddish value to be had from making that distinction. Looking at the turmoil and decline of America's largest corporations, they foresaw a world where skilled owner-operators of micro-enterprises cooperated to produce an endless variety of novel products.

Whereas the Marxists accused the Marshallians of obscuring, confusing and ultimately devaluing the role of collective ownership in the coordination of flexibility, this second school saw the emphasis on the reintegration of the economy in the society as improperly suggesting a fundamental connection between joint or community control of resources and successful innovation. Observers in this school had experience of the USA, not Germany, and, given the trade unions and state they knew, the idea that trade unions and government could create an exoskeleton of cooperation seemed outlandish in general, and just wrong in the case of the high-tech district most of them knew best – Silicon Valley. The deeper source of this objection, however, was the view, often associated with Hayek (Hayek, 1973), that all the rules and institutions needed to govern economic exchanges are created by and diffuse through the exchanges themselves. Hence any effort to 'plan' cooperation by doing through political agreement something the parties do not choose to do by contract is asking for trouble. The modern Hayekians have a single word that captures both the efficiency gains to reintegrating conception and execution and those they believe derive from respecting the distinction between economy and society: entrepreneurialism.

The difficulty with this view, in the end, proved less its dogmatism than its very disinclination for doctrine. 'Entrepreneurialism' may well have captured from the American viewpoint the dynamism of the flexible economy and the irrelevance of established institutions in their current form to it. But entrepreneurialism does not begin to describe the proliferation of joint ventures and public-private partnerships by which firms – not least in Silicon Valley – are constructing something that resembles (and may, indeed, be) an exoskeleton of cooperation. Calling all this activity an extension of normal economic transactions over extends that term; saying that it is all just an expression of entrepreneurs at work confuses the identification of an actor with an analysis of its acts. Nor does it help to invoke the idea of the new organisations as the 'formalisation' of previously informal practices. Informal organisations are usually understood as groups or networks that enable their members to correct deficiencies of the formal structure or turn its operation to their private advantage. How will informal groups set goals and monitor their own performance if they no longer operate in the shadow of formal organisations whose main purpose is to do just that? It is, in any case, indicative of this school's conviction that advances in practical activity have outstripped our languages of analysis that one of its leading writers recently published a 600-page book of episodes demonstrating the efficiency advantages of integrating conception and execution in small-scale settings (Peters, 1987). However much the Marshallians could learn about the experience of fluidity from the Hayekians they remained – rightly, I think – convinced that innovative exuberance depended on an institutional rigour that required analysis in its own right.

The third school of criticism, the Durkheimian, agreed with the Marxists in viewing the discussion of cooperation in the districts as naive. But their objection was not that cooperation in the districts was a sham. They thought it real enough. The problem, as they saw it, was that the actors in the districts and still more the observers tracing their actions misunderstood how complex, robust and organisationally self-interested the institutions of cooperation had to be in order to perform their task.

The Durkheimians' starting point is their characteristic idea that the division of labour is the precondition of economic progress, but that it undermines through specialisation the communal allegiances that define for individuals honourable callings that regulate their ambitions and give meaning to life's strivings. Only the professional associations that arise to protect the interests of new specialists but thereby make each group aware of its vulnerability to and dependence on the others provides the institutional and moral foundations of a new regulative order (Durkheim, [1893], 1984; [1950] 1992). Hence, as a conclusion, the equally characteristic Durkheimian fear that a disruption of social and economic life can lead to a disruption of associational ordering, and hence more disruption.

When the Durkheimians looked at the industrial districts, therefore, they got worried. All that cooperation on such insubstantial organisational foundations! The Durkheimians felt much more comfortable with the German variant of high-skill production: a flexible economy, as they saw it, built of large, internally decentralised firms operating under a highly codified national regulatory regime. Here powerful trade unions and employers associations were rooted in the organisationally congenial world of large corporations, whose extensive experience with internal coordination disposed them to external cooperation as well. Together these actors set and policed formal limits to non-cooperative behaviour. Above all, they established and maintained the system of skill acquisition through apprenticeship and its deployment through broad job classifications on which the flexibility of the economy ultimately depended. This system was presented both as a Northern European representative of the same genus of interpenetrating social and economic institutions of which the Italian districts were another, Mediterranean, species, and as a superior, weather-proofed development of the principles of organized economic cooperation: a rational, institutional response to chronic undersupply by unregulated markets of such public goods as certain kinds of training and rules for transactions (Streeck, 1991).

Here too important, unresolved questions were at stake. Early discussions of the districts frequently treated them as variants of a class of economy that also included the large, internally decentralised German and Japanese firms. Were the manifest differences really inconsequential? A careful comparison of the strengths and weaknesses of both systems would have deepened understanding of the connection between economic cooperation and its institutional preconditions. But the Durkheimians instead used criticism of the potential vulnerabilities of the districts as a way of exhibiting the presumed strengths of the German system. In time this exhibition hardened into a celebration of Germany as a sober utopia where a supple, resilient associational life provided the services to flexible producers that markets regularly failed to supply and less organised, more spontaneous cooperation supplied only under exceptionally fortunate circumstances.

There were, finally, any number of hybrid reactions that reverberated with the distinction between large and small firms without substantially modifying it. Schumpetarians, for instance, argued that large firms enjoyed substantial advantages in pursuing research and applying the results. Hence, other things being equal, they expected large firm variants of flexible production to do better at mastering radical, as opposed to incremental, technological changes than small ones (Lazonick, 1991). Marxists and Durkheimians were in turn drawn to this argument when it complemented their own. Similarly, the French regulation school combined elements of Marxism and Durkheimianism in order to connect the analysis of the decline of the old mass-production order to the emergence of a range of flexible alternatives, each more precisely specified than the accounts in the original discussions (Boyer *et al.*, 1986).

But even as the categories became more refined, the world spun on, to the surprise of those who had grown accustomed to having surprise on their side. So long as the organisation of production in the districts in their Italian or German variants were compared to the Fordist separation of conception and execution, they arguably exemplified the way of organising work in a post-Fordist world. Even the continuing successes of the Japanese economy did not, for a long time, require substantial revision of this view. For much of the 1970s and 1980s it seemed to many observers that Japan had perfected traditional mass-production methods in a way that allowed it to out-compete the USA without permitting it to compete directly with the districts' traditional, highly specialised and innovative niche markets.

But as Japan does so much better than expected at challenging the districts in niche markets, and American firms successfully adopt and adapt Japanese methods, these arguments become dubious. The more the inner workings of the Japanese system unfold, the more it seems to be a variant of post-Taylorism, not of mass production, and to be beating the districts at their own game: the reintegration of conception and execution. If that is so, the debates about the role of the large firm, the trade association, and the owner-operator were beside the point. Rather, as is often the case, the problem turned out to be in the understanding of what the key participants – here, the Marshallians and their Durkheimian cousins – regarded as so well understood as to be beyond discussion: the craft model of production, its limits, and possible alternatives to it. These are the themes we take up next.

The craft model and its limits

In craft production, starting in apprenticeship, the combination of practical and theoretical knowledge of related materials, tools, and techniques leads to increasing proficiency and greater autonomy in the solution of the range of problems to which all these can be applied. Groups of such specialists then cooperate in the resolution of complex tasks. The individual craftsperson is thus analogous to a versatile musician who sight-reads difficult works but also, drawing on the same underlying faculties, improvises interpretations, and the group of cooperating firms is analogous to an orchestra whose members follow a conductor's general interpretations, but would be insulted in their musicianship if instructed as to how to produce the required sounds. The connection between this broad conception of the generation and application of knowledge and the industrial organisation of the districts is so close that it was almost inevitable that students of the districts would rely – half consciously, at most – on the craft model to explain just those features of the division of labour among and within firms, as well as the social construction of the market, that escaped the conventional view.

Take first the horizontal division of labour among firms. If tasks cluster naturally into crafts, and craftspersons become more adept at solving problems within the cluster of their expertise by solving more of them, it is natural to assume that firms of craftspersons will compete by specialising in solving particular clusters of problems. Indeed, the idea that specialisation within a range of activity makes it easier and easier to solve novel problems within that range just restates and renders more precise the notion of economies of scope that accounts, we saw, for the efficiency of district firms. It also explains the loose connections among them. If firms understand their own capacities better than anyone else, and have great experience in connecting their part of a project to the whole, they, like the orchestral musicians, need only an indication of the objective as a whole to play their part. Similarly, the notion that increasing expertise goes hand in hand with increasing autonomy explains how district firms can do without internal hierarchy. If the craftspersons' skills include the capacity for self-coordination, there is no more need for coordination by plan and fiat than there is for the conductor or first chair of an orchestral section to control individual performances by annotating the score.

The social construction of the market, furthermore, is prefigured and, perhaps, even founded in the experience of apprenticeship. A central lesson of apprenticeship is that individuals must master practical knowledge of theory with the help of masters: the community of skilled workers or the craft. Only this pooled experience allows the apprentice to learn to connect the general and the particular. Hence the recognition by individuals and craft firms that autonomy is conditional on participation in the craft community that encompasses them all. Practically this means that firms must recognise the right of individuals to develop their capacities through further education or by pursuing more demanding jobs, and their own obligation as companies to support both the institutions that provide such training and an internal division of labour that accommodates those who master it. From this point of view there is nothing mysterious about the organisation of the districts as firms or the relation of the firms to each other to initiates in the mysteries of craft; and by validating the efficiency of the craft model, the districts' success could easily appear to be all but self-explanatory and limitless (see, in the spirit of self-criticism, Sabel, 1982; Piore and Sabel, 1984).

The quickening pace of innovation, however, has brought unsuspected but fundamental limits to light (Kern and Sabel, 1994). One is that the transmission of craft expertise can perversely create hierarchical obstacles to the effective, decentralised use of that expertise on the shop floor. The authority of masters over apprentices is often reproduced inside the firm as a skill hierarchy. The authority of those with greater technical expertise – technicians, foremen, and so on – to solve the technical problems that their subordinates cannot solve for themselves. Once decisions must be made amidst the flux of production on the shop floor, however, this hierarchy is paralysing. The master technicians deprecate the shop-floor solutions as technically inelegant, the shop-floor groups deplore the technical perfectionism of the higher-ups as an unaffordable luxury. In orchestras, to continue the earlier analogy, the problem is familiar as the meddlesomeness of the first chairs, who see every display of inventive virtuosity by their juniors as a challenge to their own superior rank in the hierarchy of musicianship.

At the same time the more rapid pace of innovation undermines the boundaries between groups of generalists, no matter how generally defined. Craft jurisdictions appear natural so long as the world is stable enough that an electrician's work is self-evidently different from a mechanic's. But if design and maintenance require that an 'electrician' talk incessantly with a 'mechanic,' it is unclear whether the best way to apportion tasks in any particular work group is to instruct an electrician in the relevant elements of the mechanic's craft, the mechanic in elements of the electrician's, each in the fundamentals of the other's, or a less-skilled operator with expertise in the particulars of the situation in elements of both. Relations among work groups are more complicated still. Recall the earlier example of the work group in the decentralising corporation that, being judged on its performance, has the right to solve all the problems within its reach. It can not know how far its reach extends except by extending it – trying to follow the trajectory of the solutions it elaborates, regardless of jurisdiction, until experience shows that it is overreaching. The resulting conflicts are not like scuffles for authority between students and teachers, but rather like a *Schulenstreit* among the teachers themselves. Each group of generalists has its – general – way of solving the actual problem, and wonders what combination of incomprehension, self-delusion, and arrogance allows other groups to propose alternatives. Hence the proliferation of the 'horizontal' conflicts among groups that stake out conflicting claims to general competence from the starting-point of different specialisations.

The limits of the craft model under current conditions have been most conspicuous in the German, large-firm variant of the system because it is there that apprenticeship is most fully developed and skill hierarchies and institutionalised technical specialisations most pronounced. A striking case in point is Volkswagen, a company widely seen in Germany as a pioneer in adjusting apprenticeship programmes to modern requirements. Volkswagen apprentices do come to the factory floor with a solid combination of technical and managerial or problem-solving skills. But because of the kind of hierarchical and jurisdictional conflicts just described they seldom have the chance to exercise them. The director of training at Volkswagen has called his firm a 'skills destruction machine' in print because the apprentices' general-purpose skills atrophy after a year for want of use (for references and extensive citation, see Kern and Sabel, 1994: p.612).

Indications that US subsidiaries of German firms are often having an easier time introducing work and project teams than sister plants in Germany also support the view that there is a deep connection between basic features of the craft model and current difficulties in adjusting to competition. According to US and German managers in a position to make comparisons (and who for that very reason are guarded in what they say publicly), workers who have completed apprenticeships are reluctant to accept that knowledge of the moment-to-moment flow of production – the kind of knowledge that 'semi'-skilled machine operators typically have – is relevant to the exercise of skill. They therefore resist full participation or even incorporation in work teams. In my experience, the US plants' solution to the problem is correspondingly to provide further training as required for operators working from the start in teams, rather than creating a distinct group of craft workers and then adapting their qualifications to participation in the new independent units; and I shall return below to the general implication of this response.

Evidence from the small-firm districts is scantier and more difficult to interpret, if only because turmoil in their large customers means so much turmoil for the districts that it is hard for the actors themselves to distinguish problems caused by their own shortcomings from those due to external confusion. It is striking, nonetheless, that under the pressure of new competitive standards firms in the Italian districts as well as those in Baden-Württemberg are tracing defects and delays to problems in coordination among work stations, departments or the company as a whole and its customers. Skilled operators and machines are often as flexible as could be required and as the craft model depicts them; directing and redirecting the flow of work among them turns out to be much less a matter of fact than elaboration of that same model as a set of principles governing relations within and among firms suggests it should be. Against the backdrop of such complaints the reorientation of public-sector institutions serving districts in countries such as Germany and Italy (and often cited as examples of the social construction of the market in action) is especially revealing. Until now these institutions presumed their task was to provide well-organised, flexible firms with supplemental information that they cannot provide themselves; they monitored standards, solved technical problems beyond the capabilities of small and medium-sized firms or demonstrated the capacities of new machines or software. Recently, however, they have begun to see their role as helping those firms systematise their flexibility by reexamining their internal structure and relations to their customers (see for example, Chapters 1 and 5).

To anticipate an objection: am I not confusing problems of the German or district craft systems with problems of craft systems in general? After all, there is nothing new in the observation that craft systems can be crippled by jurisdictional disputes or skill hierarchies. But some variants of the craft model address such problems much better than others, with correspondingly better economic results. Historically, for instance, the German craft economy enjoyed the flexibility permitted by broad job classifications monitored by a works council representing all employees. The British craft economy, in contrast, was hampered by narrow job classifications policed through fragile agreements between plant management and several unions representing different employee groups, often with conflicting interests. The difference was one of the main reasons why Germany outperformed Britain (Lorenz, 1993; Zeitlin, forthcoming). Why not assume, therefore, that there will probably be a new craft regime, in Germany, Italy or elsewhere, which solves the problems noted here as effectively as the current system overcomes the British debilities?

It is certainly not my intention to suggest that the limits of the craft model as I see them are incorrigible and I shall have something to say in a moment about just how the current system might jump over its shadow. But instead of speculating here on such a transformation, assessing its viability, and wondering whether still to call it a craft system, it seems more straightforward to contrast craft systems in general with an alternative method of recombining conception and execution in which skill hierarchies and jurisdictional disputes do not arise in the first place: the Japanese production system.

Learning by monitoring: overcoming the distinction between conception and execution in organisations

In contrast to the craft model, the Japanese system is based not on the extension and elaboration of skill in the sense of prowess within a technical domain. Its foundation is rather the growing capacity of the operators to improve particular operations by using the knowledge of shortcomings gained through production itself to constantly re-elaborate them (this section draws on Sabel, 1993). In executing instructions, the operators in this variant of the integration of conception and execution acquire the experience to redraw them. The division of labour is understood not, as in the craft system, as a partitioning of types of tasks, but rather as continuous revision of the responsibilities for reorganising particular activities in relation to others. One analogy here is to a theatre ensemble whose members alternate between reconceptualising their roles as a group and then exploring the possibilities and limits of each concept in the very act of performing. Another is to a jazz ensemble whose members improvise according to rules that secure the integrity of each piece, and then undertake new pieces in further exploring the improvisations (Bastien and Hostager, 1988; Brown and Duguid, 1989).

The preconditions of such joint re-elaboration of the division of labour are disciplined comparisons in which the parties are continuously comparing their possibilities to their actual capacities. This they do by connecting assessment of present to assessment of past and potential performance, or connecting evaluation of one class of solution to the evaluation of others. It is this blurring of discussion of what has been or is being done with what might be that I earlier called learning by monitoring.

In the Japanese production system the discipline required to make and refine such comparisons was historically built into the physical set-up of production by just-in-time methods that remove all buffer inventories between operations. Parts or subassemblies are produced one by one – just in time to be used by the next station or firm in the production sequence. Hence defects originating at one location are immediately apparent to the next, and the parties are constrained to discuss actual and potential problems as a precondition for producing anything at all. Whenever the system is operating smoothly, an increase in speed or the variety of output perturbs the most precarious operations and reveals the next obstacle to improvement. Preventive maintenance, statistical process controls and many other disciplines that identify possibilities for large and small improvement by locating and eliminating the sources of current difficulties are the natural results. The parties need not, however, oblige discussion by imposing such physical constraints. They can, and generally do, achieve as much by mutually fixing goals: for example, target rates of cost-cutting or

performance improvement in customer-supplier relations, or
performance criteria in projects requiring choices among competing designs (see Aoki, 1987; Smitka, 1991, Nishiguchi, 1994).

Hence the distinctive 'skill' in this system is just the ability to
learn from the flood of information about the performance of each
work station, plant, or operating unit created by moment-to-
moment stress of production to discover what does not work and
what might. 'Skill' is in quotation marks because from the perspective of the craft system this ability seems to reflect more a social
attribute dedication to the interests of the firm or the good of the
collective than a technical competence, which is, by definition,
attached to a sphere of activity, not a social entity. But observe that
the acquisition and exercise of prowess in the production-based
system, as in the craft system, moves from concrete particulars to
theoretical generalities and back. The only difference is that the
notional starting-point of this to-and-fro in the first case is a particular difficulty in production, while in the second it is an equally
concrete problem defined as technical by reference to the tools
and materials that are involved.

What is, in contrast, distinctive about the production-based
system is its rules for harmonising the individual's interest in
acquiring remunerative, socially honourable knowledge of production with the organisation's interest in inducing certain information flows. In the craft system, we saw, such harmonisation was
prefigured and initiated in apprenticeship. In Japan, school-
leavers, carefully graded according to their general abilities, pass
directly from the classroom to their first employer without broad,
practical experience of their future occupation. Hence the rules
reconciling individual and group interest are not between individuals and the community of fellows as a whole, as in a craft, but
rather between individuals and the firms that employ them. At a
minimum, no one will disclose the information required for the
mutual assessment of performance and potential in learning by
monitoring, or even tolerate disclosure by others, without assur-
ance that such disclosures will not be used at one's own expense.
Beyond that, each will want some guarantee that successful participation is rewarded.

The first rule, therefore, is to assure that even those workers
who do not expect to make innovative use of what they observe
have nothing to fear from changes induced by those who do. In
Japanese production systems as embodied in families of related
firms or *keiretsu* this is achieved by a guarantee for (full-time)

workers of long-term employment security with a substantial share of pay tied to seniority. Employees displaced by restructuring are entitled to an equivalent position in another unit of the parent corporation or an affiliated firm or subcontractor. No one, therefore, hoards information for fear of losing a job even if the prospect of advancement is poor. The second rule is to reward those who are particularly adept at learning and applying the lessons taught by observation of unbuffered production. This is done in *keiretsu* firms through a system of merit-based promotions administered by a central office – what Aoki calls the ranking hierarchy (Aoki, 1988). A central staff promotes individuals within firms according to their ability to encourage the success of work teams; the purchasing department promotes subcontractors from one supplier tier to the next according to their growing capacity to solve both their own internal problems and, with extended design capabilities, their customers'. A company union polices operation of these rules.

By these simple rules the production-based system avoids the difficulties associated with the craft model by not allowing them to arise in the first place. There is skill. But there is no skill hierarchy in the craft sense because superiors do not demonstrate exceptional prowess by solving exceptional problems with and for subordinates. Rather their defining ability is the capacity to get the production teams for which they are responsible to solve problems better themselves: it is as though the first chairs in the orchestra were responsible for encouraging improvisation in their sections.

Nor are there boundaries between groups with different substantive specialisations. In principle, all organisational distinctions are contingent and ephemeral, be they between the encompassing framework of the institution as a whole with its ranking hierarchy and pledges of employment security and the local setting of the operator in a team improving work organisation with the group and between it and others. The point to having a centralised ranking system is precisely to make the point in the way that counts most for many people: in determining their careers. Interests, of course, are specialised and everyone knows more about some things than others. But these specialisations simply determine at which locality in the organisation an operator is best placed; they are not used as a way of sorting individuals into groups that have an organisational existence of their own. Put another way, there cannot be fights among generalists in this system, as there is in the German variant of the craft model, because everyone is a generalist and no one is: everyone wants to acquire and exercise the same kind of problem-solving skills, and no one pretends to have a substantive discipline that can be extended to cover all or even most of the crucial problems in the organisation.

As you will have suspected by now, a comparison of the way the Japanese production system solves the hidden problems of craft misleadingly suggests that the Japanese system has no problems of its own, just as comparing the advantages of the craft model with the limits of Fordism misleadingly portrayed the craft system as limitless. To do justice to the complexity of the competitive balance between the craft and Japanese system, and to underscore the developmental potential of the former, I want to point to the possibility that the districts are good for yet another surprise. Even as their shortcomings become apparent, they may already be on their way to adopting some form of learning by monitoring, and one that avoids the pitfalls of the *keiretsu* system that threatens them.

Towards a new model industrial district?

The obvious limitation of the Japanese system is that it is closed. In doing away with the limiting assumption of a natural division of labour in crafts it naturalises the boundary around firm groups, thus restricting the possible forms of cooperation among operating units and the work teams of which they are composed. In doing away with the equally limiting assumption of a skills hierarchy, it creates a ranking authority whose exclusive jurisdiction gives it vast, potentially untrammeled discretion. Such a closed system works well only so long as each *keiretsu* is growing fast enough so that employees displaced in one area can be relocated in others, and expansion is lucrative enough so that central staffs and purchasing departments can reward superior performance, yet operations are still of a scale that allows these authorities to rank all they survey. But as the large firms are exposed to the increasing turbulence of world markets, their own diversification and, relatedly, their insistence that their suppliers follow suit make the *keiretsu* boundaries more obstructive. Ranking of employees, work teams, and suppliers gets more and more difficult as the ranking authorities come to depend increasingly on the views of established interlocutors in assessing the potential of newcomers and outsiders exploring the possibility of collaboration. The combination of diversification and slowing growth, furthermore, means more and more workers relocate, but fewer and fewer firms are so enfolded in any one *keiretsu* family that they will take what comes. As these burdens accumulate profits decline, and reserves are depleted. Financial strains increasingly lead firms in each group to sell the shares in the others that served as surety of observance of the common obligations. Thus as the compulsions to break the old rules grow, the constraints on doing so diminish. It is unclear whether the system will break apart under such strain, plain enough that it could.[1]

In principle, certain elements of the districts' overarching structure are well suited to house an open variant of learning by monitoring that escapes these restrictions. The open analogue to lifetime employment in the closed system is career security: the well-founded expectation that labour market experience cumulates so that a lost job can very likely be replaced with a new one. Career security in the districts is embodied in the individual's attachment to a craft, rather than a job or firm, and the employers' recognition of an obligation to provide conditions within their own firms and the district as a whole by which craft workers can acquire the skills needed to maintain employability.

The open analogue to the unitary, Japanese ranking hierarchy for promoting employees and outside collaborators is a system of multiple, competing ranking authorities. In such a system employees and suppliers can seek ranking in the hierarchy of another firm if they are unsatisfied with current treatment. Conversely, the discretion of each ranking authority is limited by competition from others. The open analogue to the Japanese company union is the territorially based labour movement that defends the interests of employees in a given area, rather than a particular firm. Indeed, precisely because the most important benefit it can offer its members is career, not job security, such a union encourages both the constant restructuring of firms and, accordingly, the constant redefinition of what should count as a generally recognised skill and how such knowledge should be acquired. Taken as a whole, the open system would be more robust than the closed one in pooling risks across more and more diverse groups and offering individuals and firms greater freedom to experiment by increasing the number of games in town.

At the most general level, such a system is, of course, characteristic of the districts. Career security is embodied in the individual's attachment to a craft, rather than a job or firm, and the employers' recognition of an obligation to provide conditions within their own firms and the district as a whole by which craft workers can acquire the skills needed to maintain employability. The presence of multiple, competing ranking hierarchies is manifest in the mobility of workers among firms and the constant reordering of subcontracting relations, by which the lead firm and supplier on one project can trade places on the next. Territorial unions are the rule, not the exception, in the districts; lost work sites are too small to support the costs of a full-time union official to negotiate and administer contracts. In any case employers themselves have an interest in a district-wide organisation that protects each firm, and the reputation of the region as a whole, against those who would compete by violating standards.

But if the advantages of the districts' open institutions are obvious, so is it equally obvious that they are advantageous only in principle because of their continuing attachment to craft. If the deployment and development of skill is limited by skill hierarchies and jurisdictional conflicts, then firms will not know whom to reward for what, and successful craft careers, shaped by the territorial union, will not necessarily result in career security. So, moving still in the realm of the obvious, the last and crucial question is: can the districts retain their openness while relaxing the connection to craft sufficiently to allow experimenting with the forms of cooperation that I am calling learning by monitoring?

The answer, I think, is that they are doing so already through a combination of organisational reforms, reorientation of the provision of real services by district institutions, changes in training, and reconsideration of the provision of social welfare funds and services at the local level. Of these, the organisational changes are the preconditions for the others. Recall that the districts' difficulties have less to do with an absolute incapacity to master any particular task than with jurisdictional struggles that prevent determination of what needs to be done and who should do it. Any resolution of such struggles that ends not in stalemate but in identification of a more effective organisation of work provides important clues to and helps create the foundations for subsequent steps. Managers and entrepreneurs in the districts are well aware of this; and for the last several years they have let the contestants in such conflicts fight to the finish in order to determine what they themselves should do next. More recently still, district unions have begun to regard these conflicts as part and parcel of restructuring, rather than as temporary disturbances of normalcy.

As the earlier reference to the decentralising corporation suggested, the crucial organisational reform in this regard is simply to judge work groups or operating units by their results and give them sufficient freedom so that their performance actually depends on their decisions. This reform is doubly appealing in the districts as it allows the crafts to sort out their own jurisdictional problems while institutionalising the cardinal principle of the Japanese system and learning by monitoring in general: those closest to the flux of information generated by production should have a central voice in its reorganisation. Such reforms are, of course, disruptive and potentially dangerous to those who initiate them. Work teams and operating units may in effect fire their supervisors by providing themselves or purchasing from outsiders services that those supervisors furnished; and decentralisation may eventually undermine the integrity of the firm as teams cooperate more with outsiders than with internal units. Factory councils and unions may lose their influence as the boundaries of the firms become blurry. For these reasons thoroughgoing decentralisation is a last resort. But by the same token, once begun, as it apparently has in many districts and large corporations, it is hard to stop, and likely to provoke collateral, self-reinforcing changes in district institutions.

One of the most important of these changes is the reorientation of real services noted earlier. Restructuring firms that are changing everything step by step need advice about where to start and how to accomplish each stage. As it is well established in districts that public institutions can provide information on best practice that firms cannot sort out for themselves, firms are turning to established providers of real services for help in understanding the new, decentralised structures of authority in general and the separate disciplines of quality control, just-in-time delivery that ensure rigour in the discussions that reform makes possible. Thus officials of the Steinbeis Stiftung, which distinguished itself as a leader of technology transfer in Baden-Württemberg, talk quietly of the need to provide more 'intimate' services in connection with the internal reorganisation of local firms, and regional trade unions are participating in numerous discussions of various ways to achieve this end.[2]

A further, less conspicuous, but perhaps more consequential reform concerns vocational training. Apprenticeship and vocational training more generally have long been the districts' pride for reasons connected to their craft heritage. Recently, however, the emphasis has begun to shift from training of workers in established technical disciplines to the instruction of managers in the new principles of decentralised operation with work teams and units, and away from formal training in general to the acquisition of know-how on the job. This is done, for example, by the introduction of pay-for-knowledge. As its name suggests, this is a system of compensation that rewards employees for what they can demonstrably do at work rather than for, say, educational certificates or seniority they have earned. Pay-for knowledge facilitates the introduction of work teams by allowing groups to define tasks and rewards as local experience warrants. Conversely, it undercuts the power of craft as a guiding principle in the organisation of firms and individual careers by underscoring the extent to which the knowledge that counts and the ability to evaluate it must be tied to the experience of production itself. Unions have been hesitant to endorse these changes in advance of some understanding of their role in some potential successor to the old vocational system; but given their concerns in this regard, it is remarkable that they tolerate as much experimentation as they do.

Finally, there is the matter of local welfare reform. The massive reorganisation of firms and the disruption of individual lives that it provokes in the districts burdens social welfare funds when they are already strained to the breaking point. Increasingly, the districts' response is to make more efficient use of resources by pooling monies from different programmes to address problems – the closing of a particular plant, or the reorientation of a whole sector – as wholes, and to supplement national systems with local self-insurance. This raises complex questions of moral hazard: what is to prevent the district from using waivers it obtains of national rules to plunder the national coffers? How will the residents of the district be protected against the possibility of self-dealing on the part of those who administer the local welfare funds? I take it as a sign of the continuing institutional integrity of districts in Emilia-Romagna, Jutland and elsewhere that these questions are openly addressed by employers and unions alike in the interest of finding a way to pool the risks of adjustment.

It is of course impossible to predict whether all of these changes will cohere into a new, open district system. Perhaps the Germans, with their larger firms and highly formalised system of apprenticeship, will have a harder time of it than the Italians or Danes with their smaller firms and more supple systems – informal in the former case, well institutionalised in the latter – of blending continuing education with on-the-job training that crosses and constantly redefines craft lines. Perhaps Silicon Valley, with its vast experience with networked firms and its indifference to craft traditions, will have an easier time still (Saxenian, 1994). Perhaps at the end of the day the operation of a reorganised district will be governed by the same principles as that of a decentralised large firm; perhaps, too, national economies will come to be seen as federations of regional ones. But if history is any guide, then the one thing beyond doubt is that the districts will reinvent themselves, retaining a family resemblance to their craft past while creating something fundamentally novel – the model, perhaps, both of the entity that comes to supplant the firm as the basal unit of the micro-economy and the national state as the instrument of macro-economic control. Just watch them.

Notes

1. This section schematises my current research on restructuring in the USA, Japan and Western Europe. References to the districts reflect many conversations with Sebastiano Brusco, Peer Hull Kristensen, and Gary Herrigel, with whom I am collaborating on a project on economic adjustment in Baden-Württemberg. A first treatment is Sabel (1994).
2. For an overview of current restructuring in Baden-Württemberg, with emphasis on new efforts to encourage reorganisation within firms, see Kern (1994).

SELECT BIBLIOGRAPHY

Alba, A., 'El empleo autonómo en una economía con empleo masivo', *Economía Industrial*, 284:59–69, 1992.

Allen, G. C., *The Industrial Development of Birmingham and the Black Country, 1860–1927*, London, 1929.

Allen, Robert C., 'Collective invention', *Journal of Economic Behavior and Organization*, 4:1–24, 1983.

Amar, M., 'Dans l'industrie, les PME résistent mieux que les grandes enterprises', *Économie et Statistique*, 197:3–12, 1987.

Amin, A. and Robins, K., 'Industrial districts and regional development: limits and possibilities', in F. Pyke, G. Beccattini and W. Sengenberger, *International Districts and Inter-firm Cooperation in Italy*, Geneva, International Institute for Labour Studies, 1990.

Amin, Ash and Smith, Ian, 'Vertical integration or disintegration? The case of the UK car parts industry', in Christopher M. Law (ed.), *Restructuring the Global Automobile Industry*, London, Routledge, 1991.

Antonelli, C. (ed.), *New Information Technology and Industrial Change: the Italian Case*, Dordrecht, Kluver Academic Publishers, 1988.

Aoki, M., 'Innovative adaptation through the quasi-tree structure', *Zeitschrift für Nationalokönomie*, 44:177–88, 1987.

Aoki, M., *Information, Incentives, and Bargaining in the Japanese Economy*, Cambridge, Cambridge University Press, 1988.

Bagnasco, A., 'La costruzione sociale del mercato: strategie di impresa e esperimenti di scale in Italià', *Stato e Mercato*:9–45, 1985.

——, *La costruzione sociale del mercato*, Bologna, Il Mulino, 1988.

Bagnasco, A. and Trigilia, C. (eds), *Società e politica nelle aree di piccola impres: Il caso di Bassano*, Venice, Arsenale, 1984.

——, *Società e politica nelle aree di piccola impresa: Il caso della Valdelsa*, Milan, Angeli, 1985.

——, *La construction sociale du marché. Le defi de la troisième Italie*, Paris, Les Editions de L'Ecole Normale Supérieure du Cachan, 1993.

Banville, E. (de), 'L'entreprise entre la PMI-sation et l'évolution des reseaux de solidarité', Rapport Cresal, multigr, 1984.

Barber, J., Metcalfe, J. S. and Porteous, M. (eds), *Barriers to Growth in Small Firms*, London, Routledge, 1989.

Bastien, D. T. and Hostager, T. J., 'Jazz as a process of organizational innovation', *Communication Research*, 15: 582–602.

Becattini, G. (ed.), *Mercato e forze locale: il distretto industriale*, Bologna, Il Mulino, 1987.

——, 'Sectors and/or districts: some remarks on the conceptual foundations of industrial economics', in E. Goodman, J. Bamford, with Peter Saynor (eds), *Small Firms and Industrial Districts in Italy*, London, Routledge, 1989.

——, 'The Marshallian industrial district as a socio-economic notion', in F. Pyke, G. Becattini and W. Sengenberger, *International Districts and Inter-firm Cooperation in Italy*, Geneva, International Institute for Labour Studies, 1990.

Bechtle, G., Düll, N., Kuhn, H. and Wex, T., 'Arbeit und Unternehmen in den starken Regionen Europas, Der Fall Baden-Württemberg', mimeo, Munich, ISF, 1992.

Beckouche, P., Savy, M. and Veltz, P., 'Nouvelle économie, nouveaux territoires', in Caisse des Dépôts et Consignations, *Économie et territoire: vers une nouvelle dynamique du développement local*, vol. 2, multigr, 1986.

Bellandi, M., 'The industrial district in Marshall', in E. Goodman, J. Bamford, with Peter Saynor (eds), *Small Firms and Industrial Districts in Italy*, London, Routledge, 1989.

Benko, G. and Lipietz, A., *Les régions qui gagnent: districts et réseaux: les nouveaux paradigmes de la géographie économique*, Paris, PUF, 1992.

Benton, L. 'The emergence of industrial districts in Spain: industrial restructuring and diverging regional responses', in F. Pyke and W. Sengenberger (eds), *Industrial Districts and Local Economic Regeneration*, Geneva, International Institute of Labour Studies, 1992.

Berger, S., 'The traditional sector in France and Italy', in Suzanne Berger and Michael Piore, *Dualism and Discontinuity in Industrial Societies*, Cambridge, Cambridge University Press, 1980.

Bericat, E., 'Distritos y nebulosas industriales', *Sociologia del Trabajo*, 11:49–66, 1990–91.

Bernschneider, W., Schindler, M. G. and Schüller, J., 'Industriepolitik in Baden-Württemberg und Bayern', in U. Jürgens and W. Krumbein (eds), *Industriepolitische Strategien. Bundesländer im Vergleich*, Berlin, Sigma, 1991.

Blackbourn, David and Eley, Geoff, *The Peculiarities of German History*, Oxford. Oxford University Press, 1984.

Bonin, H., *Histoire économique de la France depuis 1880*, Paris, Masson, 1988.

Boyer, R. (ed.), *Capitalismes fin de siècle*, Paris, PUF, 1986.

Brown, J. S. and Duguid, P., 'Learning and improvisation: local sources of global innovation', unpublished manuscript, 1989.

Brown, W. (ed.), *The Changing Contours of British Industrial Relations*, Oxford, Blackwell, 1980.

Brown, W. and Walsh, J., 'Pay determination in Britain in the 1980s: the anatomy of decentralization', *Oxford Review of Economic Policy*, 7, 1:44–59, 1991.

Brusco, S., 'The Emilian model: productive decentralization and social integration', *Cambridge Journal of Economics*, 6:167–84, 1982.

—, 'Small firms and industrial districts: the experience of Italy', in D. Keeble and E. Wever (eds), *New Firms and Regional Developments in Europe*, London, Croom Helm, 1986.

—, *Piccole imprese e distretti industriali*, Turin, Rosenberg & Sellier, 1989.

—, 'The idea of industrial district: its genesis', in F. Pyke, G. Becattini and W. Sengenberger, *International Districts and Inter-firm Cooperation in Italy*, Geneva, International Institute for Labour Studies, 1990.

—, 'Small firms and the provision of real services' in F. Pyke and W. Sengenberger (eds), *Industrial Districts and Social–Economic Regeneration*, Geneva, International Institute of Labour Studies, 1992.

Bucaille, A. and Costa de Beauregard, B., *PMI, enjeux régionaux et internationaux*, Paris, Economica, 1987.

Capie, Forrest and Rodrik–Bali, Ghila, 'Concentration in British banking, 1870–1920', *Business History*, 24:280–92, 1982.

Castillo, J. J., *La división del trabajo entre empresas*, Madrid, Ministerio de Trabajo y SS, 1989.

—, *Informatizacion, Trabajo y Empleo en las pequeñas empresas españolas*, Madrid, Ministerio de Trabajo y SS, 1991.

Cento Bull, A., Pitt, M. and Szarka, J., 'Small firms and industrial districts, structural explanations of small firm viability in three countries', *Entrepreneurship and Regional Development*, 3:83–99, 1991.

Chandler, J. and Alfred, D., *The Visible Hand: The Managerial Revolution in American Business*, Cambridge, Harvard University Press, 1977.

Channon, Derek F., *Strategy and Structure of British Enterprise*, Boston, MA, Harvard Business School Press, 1973.

Cohen, E., *L'État-brancardier: politiques du déclin industriel (1974–1984)*, Paris, Calmann-Levy, 1989.

Collins, Michael, *Money and Banking in the UK: A History*, London, Routledge, 1988.

—, *Banks and Industrial Finance in Britain, 1800–1939*, London, Macmillan, 1991.

Cooke, P. H., and Morgan, K., *Industry, training and technology transfer: the Baden–Württemberg system in perspective*, Regional Industrial Research Report, Cardiff, University of Wales, Department of City and Regional Planning, 1990.

—, 'Growth regions under duress: renewal strategies in Baden–Württemberg and Emilia–Romagna', in A. Amin and N. Thrift (eds), *Holding Down the Global: Possibilities for Local Economic Policy*, 1993.

Cosh, A. D., Hughes, A., Lee, K., and Singh, A., 'Institutional investment, mergers and the market for corporate control', *International Journal of Industrial Organization*, 7:73–100, 1989.

Costa Campi, M. T., 'Cambios en la organizacíon industrial: cooperacíon local y competitividad internacional. Panorama general', *Economía Industrial*, 286:19–36, 1992.

Cottrell, P. L., 'The domestic commercial bank and the City of London, 1870–1939', in Y. Cassis (ed.), *Finance and Financiers in European History, 1880–1960*, Cambridge, Cambridge University Press, 1992.

Courlet, C1. and Judet, P., 'Nouveaux espaces de production en France et en Italie', *Les Annales de la Recherche Urbaine*, 291:95–103. 1986.

Crewe, L. and Davenport, E., 'The puppet show: changing buyer-supplier relationships within clothing retailing', *Transactions of the Institute of British Geographers*, 17:183–97, 1992.

Crossick, Geoffrey and Haupt, Hans–Gerhard (eds), *Shopkeepers and Master Artisans in Nineteenth–Century Europe*, London, Methuen, 1984.

Crouch, C. and Marquand, D. (eds), *The New Centralism: Britain Out of Step in Europe?*, Oxford, Blackwell, 1989.

Dammgaard, Ellen, *Peder Lykke. En Husmand på Heden*, Copenhagen, Nyt Nordisk Forlag, Arnold Bucck, 1983.

Dore, R., *Flexible Rigidities*, Stanford, Stanford University Press, 1986.

Dunne, P. and Hughes, A., 'Small businesses: an analysis of recent trends in their relative importance and growth performance in the UK with some European comparisons', working paper 1, Cambridge, Small Business Research Centre, University of Cambridge, 1990.

Dupree, Margaret, 'The cotton industry: a middle way between nationalisation and self-government?', in Helen Mercer, Neil Rollings and Jim Tomlinson (eds), *Labour Governments and Private Industry: The experience of 1945–51*, Edinburgh. Edinburgh University Press, 1992.

Durkheim, E.. *The Division of Labour in Society*, New York, Free Press, 1984 [1st ed. 1893].

—, *Professional Ethics and Civic Morals*, New York. Routledge, 1992 [1st ed. 1950].

Edwards, Ronald S., *Co-operative Industrial Research*, London, Pitman, 1950.

Fairburn, John and Kay, J. A. (eds). *Mergers and Merger Policy*, Oxford, Oxford University Press, 1989.

Fitzgerald, Robert, *British Labour Management and Industrial Welfare*, 1846–1939, London, Croom Helm, 1987.

Forsgren, M. and Johanson, J., *Internationall Foretagsekonomi*, Stockholm, Nordstedts, 1975.

Ganne, B., *Industrialisation diffuse et systèmes industriels localisés: essai de bibliographique critique du cas français*, Geneva, International Institute of Social Studies, ILO, Bibliographical Series, 14. 1990.

Gapper, Michael, 'Small business: banks rethink lending policy', *Financial Times*, corporate finance supplement, 19 July: iv, 1993.

Goldthorpe, J. H., *Social Mobility and Class Structure in Modern America*, Oxford, Clarendon Press, 1980.

— (ed.), *Order and Conflict in Contemporary Capitalism. Studies in the Political Economy of Western European Nations*, Oxford, Oxford University Press, 1984.

Goold, Michael and Campbell, Andrew, *Strategies and Styles: the Role of the Centre in Managing Diversified Corporations*, Oxford, Blackwell.

Grant, Wyn with Sargent, Jane, *Business and Politics in Britain*, London, Macmillan, 1987.

Gremion, P., *Le pouvoir périphérique: bureaucrates et notables dans le système politique français*, Paris, Le Seuil, coll. sociologie, 1976.

Grøn, J. H., *Arbejde-Virksomheder-Regioner*, Esbjerg, Sudjysk Universitetsforlag, 1985.

Hall, Graham. 'Lack of finance as a constraint on the expansion of innovatory small firms', in J. Barber, J. S. Metcalfe and M. Porteous (eds), *Barriers to Growth in Small Firms*, London, Routledge, 1989.

Hall, Peter. *The Industries of London Since 1861*, London, 1961.

—, *Governing the Economy: The Politics of State Intervention in Britain and France*, Cambridge, Polity, 1986.

Hannah, Leslie, *the Rise of the Corporate Economy*, 2nd ed., London, Methuen, 1983.

Harrison, B., 'Are industrial clusters losing their luster?', *Technology Review*, 97:66, 1994.

Hayek, F., *Law, Legislation and Liberty: A New Statement of the Liberal Principles of Justice and Political Economy*, vol. 1, *Rules and Order*, Chicago, University of Chicago Press, 1973.

Head, P., 'Boots and shoes', in Derek H. Aldcroft (ed.), *The Development of British Industry and Foreign Competition*, 1875–1914, London, Allen & Unwin, 1968.

Henderson, P. D., 'Development councils: an industrial experiment', in G. D. N. Worswick and P. H. Ady (eds), *The British Economy, 1945–50*, 1952.

Herrigel, G., 'Industrial organization and the politics of industry: centralized and decentralized production in Germany', PhD dissertation, Boston, MIT. Department of Political Science, 1990.

Hill, C. W. L. and Pickering, J. F., 'Divisionalization, decentralization and performance of large United Kingdom companies', *Journal of Management Studies*, 23: 26–50, 1986.

Hirst, P. and Zeitlin, J. (eds), *Reversing Industrial Decline? Industrial Structure and Policy in Britain and Her Competitors*, Oxford, Berg, 1989a.

—, 'Flexible specialisation and the competitive failure of UK manu-facturing', *Political Quarterly*, 60:164–78, 1989b.

—, 'Flexible specialization vs, post-Fordism: theory, evidence and policy implications', *Economy and Society*, 20:1–55, 1991.

Hofmann, J., 'Innovationsförderung in Berlin und Baden-Württemberg – Zum regionalen Eigenleben technologiepolitis-cher Konzepte', in U. Jürgens and W. Krumbein (eds). *Industriepolitische Strategien. Bundesländer im Vergleich*, Berlin, Sigman, 1991.

Høpner-Petersen, J., *Case study: UNIBANK A/S Herning. Bankradgiveres efteruddanelse i en centerfilial*. Copenhagen, 10A, Copenhagen Business School, 1992.

Houssel, J. P., 'Les industries autochtones en milieu rural', *Revue de Géographie de Lyon*, 4:304–41, 1980.

Houssel, J. P. *et al.*, 'L'industrialisation en milieu rural dans la région Rhône-Alpes', *Revue de Géographie de Lyon*, 67, 3, 1992.

Hughes, Alan, 'Small firms' merger activity and competition policy', in J. Barber. J. S. Metcalfe and M. Porteous (eds), *Barriers to Growth in Small Firms*, London, Routledge, 1989.

IMADE, *Institute Madrileño de Desarrolllo, Objetivos, Estrategia, Programas*, Madrid, IMADE, 1992.

Jenkins, David T. and Ponting, Kenneth G., *The British Wool Textile Industry, 1770–1914*, London, Scolar Press, 1982.

Jones, B. and Saren, M., 'Politics and institutions in small business development: comparing Britain and Italy', *Labour and Society*, 15:287–300, 1990.

Kern, H., 'Intelligente Regulierung: Gewerkschaftliche Beiträge in Ost und West zur Erneuerung des deutschen Produktionsmodells', *Soziale Welt*, 1:33–59, 1994.

Kern, H. and Sabel, C. F., 'Verblasste Tugenden. Zur Krise des deutschen Produktionsmodells', in N. Beckenbach and W. V. Treeck (eds), *Umbrüche gesellschaftlicher Arbeit, N.*, Göttingen, Verlag Otto Schwartz & Co., 1994.

Kjeldsen-Kragh, S., *Specialisering og Konkurrenceevne*, Copenhagen, 1973.

Kristensen, P. H., 'Strategies against structure, institutions and economic organization in Denmark', in R. Whitley (ed.), *European Business Systems, Firms and Markets in their National Context*, London, Sage, 1992a.

——, 'Industrial districts in West Jutland, Denmark', in F. Pyke and W. Sengenberger (eds), *Industrial Districts and Local*

Economic Regeneration, Geneva, International Institute of Labour Studies, 1992b.

——, 'Local system building and policy at national and European level', *Vocational Training*: 27–31, 1992c.

——, 'Strategies in a volatile world', paper presented at European Business System Group's workshop 'The Changing Nature of European Business Systems', Helsinki, February. 1993a.

——, 'Case study: APV-Rosista, Horsens. Structured continuing training in a volatile economy', Berlin, Cedefop, 1993b.

Kristensen. P. H. and Sabel, C., 'The small-holder economy in Denmark, the exception as variation', in C. F. Sabel and J. Zeitlin (eds), *Worlds of Possibility, Flexibility and Mass Production in Western Industrialization*, 1993.

Kuisel, R. F., *Le capitalisme et l'Etat en France, modernisation et dirigisme au XXe siècle*, Paris, 1984.

Laborie, J. P., Langumier, J. F., and De Roo, P., *La politique française d'aménagement du Territoire de 1950 à 1985*, Paris, La Documentation Française, 1985.

Lane, C., 'European business systems: Britain and Germany compared'. in R. Whitley (ed.), *European Business Systems. Firms and Markets in their National Context*, London, Sage, 1992.

Lazonick, W., *Business Organization and the Myth of the Market Economy*, New York, Cambridge University Press, 1991.

Lockwood, D., 'Sources of variations in working-class images of society', *Sociological Review*, 3, 1966.

Lorenz, Edward H., *Economic Decline in Britain: The Shipbuilding Industry, 1890–1970*, Oxford, Clarendon Press, 1991.

——, 'Economic decline in twentieth-century Britain: the cotton, shipbuilding and car industries', Paris, University of Notre Dame, 1993.

Loveman, Gary and Sengenberger, Werner, 'Introduction – economic and social reorganisation in the small and medium-sized enterprise sector', in Werner Sengenberger, Gary Loveman and Michael J. Piore (eds), *The Re-emergence of Small Enterprises*, Geneva, International Institute for Labour Studies, 1990.

Lovering, John, 'The local economy and local economic strategies', *Policy and Politics*, 16:145–57, 1988.

McCrone, Gavin, *Regional Policy in Britain*, London, Allen & Unwin, 1969.

Magatti, M., *Mercato e forze sociali. Due distretti tessile: Lancashire e Ticino Olona, 1950–1980*, Bologna, Il Mulino, 1991.

Maier, H. E., 'Das Modell Baden-Württemberg. Über institutionelle Voraussetzungen differenzierter Qualitätsproduktion', working paper, Berlin, Wissenschaftszetrum, 1987.

Marshall, Alfred, Principles of Economics, 8th ed., London, Macmillan, 1992 [1st ed. 1890].

——, Industry and Trade, London, Macmillan, 1927 [1st ed. 1919].

——, The Early Economic Writings of Alfred Marshall, 1867–1890, vol. 2, J. K. Whitaker (ed.), London, Macmillan, 1975.

Maskell, P., Nyetableringer i Industrien – Og Industristrukturens Udvikling, Copenhagen, Handelshojskølens Forlag, 1992.

Mercer, H., 'The Labour governments of 1945–51 and private industry', in N. Tiratsoo (ed.), The Attlee Years, London, Pinter, 1991.

Ministère du Plan et de l'aménagement du Territoire, Le développement des PME–PMI en France: l'industrie au futur', Paris, La Documentation Française, 1983.

Nishiguchi, T., Strategic Industrial Sourcing: The Japanese Advantage, New York, Oxford University Press, 1994.

O'Brien. Patrick and Keyder, Caglar, Economic Growth in France and Britain. 1780–1914, London, Allen & Unwin, 1978.

Oliver, J. L., The Structure and Development of the Furniture Industry, New York, 1966.

Pagden, A., 'The destruction of trust and its economic consequences in the case of eighteenth-century Naples', in D. Gambetta (ed.), Trust. Making and Breaking Cooperative Relations, New York, Basil Blackwell, 1988.

Parkin F., Class Inequality and Political Order, London, MacGibbon & Kee, 1971.

Penn, R., 'Contemporary relationships between firms in a classical industrial locality: evidence from the social change and economic initiative', Work. Employment and Society, 6:209–27, 1992.

Perulli, P., 'Il distretto di Modena', in M. Regini and C. Sabel (eds), Strategie di riagginstamento industriale, Bologna, Il Mulino, 1989.

Peters, T., Thriving on Chaos: Handbook for a Management Revolution, New York, Knopf, 1987.

Piore, M. J. and Sabel, C. F., The Second Industrial Divide, Possibilities for Prosperity, New York, Basic Books, 1984.

Polanyi, K., The Great Transformation, New York, Rinehart & Winston, 1944.

Pollard, Sidney, *Britain's Prime and Britain's Decline: The British Economy, 1870–1914*, London, Edward Arnold, 1989.

Pyke, Frank, 'Co-operation and control in a northern woman's town', working paper, Manchester, North West Industrial Research Unit, University of Manchester, 1987a.

—— 'Industrial networks and modes of co-operation in a British context', working paper, Manchester, North West Industrial Research Unit, University of Manchester, 1987b.

—— 'Co-operative practices among small and medium-sized establishments', – *Work, Employment and Society*, 2:352–65, 1988.

—— 'Strengthening small firms through co-operation and technical services: the roles of the Steinbeis Foundation and the Landesgewerbeamt in Baden-Württemberg', Background Paper no. 2 for the International Conference on Endogenous Regional Development in a Global Economy, Valencia, 17–19 November 1992.

Pyke, F., Becattini, G. and Sengenberger, W., *International Districts and Inter-firm Cooperation in Italy*, Geneva, International Institute for Labour Studies, 1990.

Pyke, F. and Sengenberger, W. (eds), *Industrial Districts and Local Economic Regeneration*, Geneva, International Institute of Labour Studies, 1992.

Rico, A., 'Politica industrial, servicios y regiones', *Economía Industrial*, 286:123–35, 1992.

Rubery, J., Tarling, R. and Wilkinson, F., 'Flexibility, marketing and the organisation of production', *Labour and Society*, 12: 131–51, 1987.

Rubery, J. and Wilkinson, F., 'Distribution, flexibility of production and the British footwear industry', *Labour and Society*, 14: 121–40, 1989.

Sabel, C. F., *Work and Politics: the Division of Labour in Industry*, Cambridge, Cambridge University Press, 1982.

—— 'Flexible specialisation and the re-emergence of regional economies', in P. Hirst and J. Zeitlin (eds), *Reversing Industrial Decline? Industrial Structure and Policy in Britain and her Competitors*, Oxford, Berg, 1989.

—— 'Studied trust, building new forms of co-operation in a volatile economy', in F. Pyke and W. Sengenberger (eds), *Industrial Districts and Local Economic Regeneration*, Geneva, International Institute of Labour Studies, 1992.

—— 'Learning by monitoring: the institutions of economic development', in N. Smelser and R. Swedberg (eds), *Handbook of Economic Sociology*, Princeton, NJ, Princeton-Sage, 1993.

—— 'Bootstrapping reform: rebuilding firms, the welfare state and unions', unpublished manuscript, Massuchusetts Institute of Technology, Department of Political Science, 1994.

Sabel, C. F. and Zeitlin, J., 'Alternative storiche alla produzione di massa', *Stato e Mercato*, 5:212–58, 1982.

—— 'Historical alternatives to mass production: politics, markets and technology in nineteenth-century industrialisation', *Past and Present*, 108: 133–76, 1985.

Sako, M., *Prices, Quality and Trust: Inter-firm Relations in Britain and Japan*, Cambridge, Cambridge University Press, 1992.

Sanchez Lopez, A. J., 'Estrategias e instrumentos de las iniciativas locales de fomento económio (en Andalucía)', *Sociología* del Trabajo, 14:68–89, 1991–2.

Sanchis, E., *et al.*, 'La nueva pequeña empresa de la industria valenciana', *Sociología del Trabajo*, 5:41–65, 1988–9.

Sauvy, A., *Histoire économique de la France entre les deux guerres*, vol. 2, Paris, Economica, 1984.

Saxenian, A., 'The Cheshire Cat's grin: innovation, regional development and the Cambridge case', *Economy and Society*: 448–77, 1989.

——, *Regional Advantage: Culture and Competition in Silicon Valley and Route 128*, Cambridge, MA, Harvard University Press, 1994.

Schmitz, H., 'Industrial districts: model and reality in Baden-Württemberg', in F. Pyke and W. Sengenberger (eds), *Industrial Districts and Local Economic Regeneration*, Geneva, ILO, 1992.

Scott, A. J. and Paul, A., 'Collective order and economic coordination in industrial agglomerations: the technopoles of southern California', *Environment and Planning C: Government and Policy*, 8:179–93, 1990.

Semlinger, K., 'Innovation, cooperation and strategic contracting', International conference 'Management of Technology', Paris, 27–28 May, mimeo, Munich, ISF, 1991a.

—, 'A marketing approach for public intervention into enterprise decision making', Tenth EGOS-Colloquium on 'Societal Change Between Markets and Organization', Vienna, 15–17 July, mimeo, Munich, ISF, 1991b.

—, 'Effizienz und Autonomie in Zulieferungsnetzwerken, Zum Strategischen Gehalt von Kooperation', in W. H. Staehle and J. Sydow (eds), *Management forschung*, vol. 3, Berlin and New York, Walter de Gruyter: 309–54, 1993.

Smith, A., *The Wealth of Nations*, Chicago, University of Chicago Press, 1976 [1st ed. 1776].

Smitka, M. J., *Competitive Ties: Subcontracting in the Japanese Automobile Industry*, New York, Columbia University Press, 1991.

Sociologie du Travail, *Sociologie du 'local' et 'relocalisation' du social*, 3, 1983.

—, *Les acteurs du développement local*, 4, 1991.

Sombart, W., *Why Is There No Socialism in the United States?*, London, Macmillan, 1976 [1st ed. 1906].

Storey, D. J. and Johnson, S., *Job Generation and Labour Market Change*, London, Macmillan, 1987.

Storper, M. and Harrison, B., 'Flexibility, hierarchy and regional development: the changing structure of production systems and their forms of governance in the 1900s', *Research Policy*, 20: 407–22, 1991.

Strandskov, J., *Hvor Internationale er Danske Virksomheder?*, Copenhagen, Forlaget Management/Samfundslitteratur, 1987.

Streeck, W., 'On the institutional conditions of diversified quality production', in E. Mazner and W. Streeck (eds), *The Socio-Economics of Production and Employment*, London, Edward Elgar, 1991.

—, 'The logics of associative action and the territorial organization of interests: the case of German *Handwerk*', in W. Streeck, *Social Institutions and Economic Performance*, London, Sage, 1992.

Tarling, R. and Wilkinson, F., 'The movement of real wages and the development of collective bargaining in the UK, 1855–1920', *Contributions to Political Economy*, 1:1–23.

Thomas, W. A., *The Provincial Stock Exchanges*, London, Frank Cass, 1973.

Thoms, David and Donnelly, Tom, *The Motor Car Industry in Coventry since the 1890s*, London, Croom Helm, 1985.

Tolliday, Steven, *Business, Banking, and Politics. The Case of British Steel, 1918–1939*, Cambridge, MA, Harvard University Press, 1987.

Tolliday, Steven and Zeitlin, Jonathan (eds), *The Power to Manage? Employers and Industrial Relations in Comparative Historical Perspective*, London, Routledge, 1991.

Travers, Tony, 'The threat to the autonomy of elected local government', in C. Crouch and D. Marquand (eds), *The New Centralism: Britain Out of Step in Europe?*, Oxford, Blackwell, 1989.

Trigilia, Carlo, *Grandi partiti e piccole imprese*, Bologna, Il Mulino, 1986.

—, 'Work and politics in the Third Italy', in F. Pyke, G. Becattini and W. Sengenberger (eds), *Industrial Districts and Inter-Firm Co-operation in Italy*, Geneva, International Institute for Labour Studies, 1990.

—, 'The paradox of the region: economic regulation and the representation of interests', *Economics and Society*, 20:306–27, 1991.

—, 'Italian industrial districts: neither myth nor interlude', in F. Pyke and W. Sengenberger, *Industrial Districts and Local Economic Regeneration*, Geneva, International Institute of Labour Studies, 1992.

Turnbull, P., 'Buyer-supplier relations in the UK automotive industry', in Blyton and Morris, 1991.

Varcoe, Ian, 'Co-operative research associations in British industry, 1918–34', *Minerva*, 19:433–63, 1981.

Walsh, Janet, 'The performance of UK textiles and clothing: recent controversies and evidence', *International Review of Applied Economics*, 5:277–309, 1991.

Weiss, Linda, *Creating Capitalism: Small Business and the State since 1945*, Oxford, Blackwell, 1988.

Wells, F. A., *The British Hosiery and Knitwear Industry*, rev. ed., Newton Abbott, David Charles [1st ed. 1935].

Whipp, Richard, *Patterns of Labour: Work and Social Change in the Pottery Industry*, London, Routledge, 1990.

Whitaker, Marian, 'Towards flexibility: technical change and buyer supplier relations in the British clothing industry', in Blyton and Morris, 1991.

Whitley, R. (ed.), *European Business Systems, Firms and Markets in their National Context*, London, Sage, 1992.

Williams, K., Williams, J. and Thomas, D., *Why are the British Bad at Manufacturing?*, London, Routledge and Kegan Paul, 1983.

Williamson, O. E., *The Economic Institutions of Capitalism: Firms, Markets, Relational Contacts*, New York, The Free Press, 1985.

Worms, J. P., 'Le préfet et ses notables', *Sociologie du travail*, 3, 1966.

Wray, Margaret, *The Women's Outerwear Industry*, London, Duckworth, 1957.

Young, Stephen with Love, A. V., *Intervention in the Mixed Economy: The Evolution of British Industrial Policy, 1964–72*, London, Croom Helm.

Zdatny, Steven, *The Politics of Survival: Artisans in Twentieth-Century France*, Oxford, Oxford University Press, 1990.